BARBADOS

By the same author

1 (overleaf) Coconut palm trees on Powell Spring Beach, facing the Atlantic on the East Coast

George Hunte

BARBADOS

Hastings House Publishers
New York NY10016

First published 1974

© copyright George Hunte 1974

Printed in Great Britain

Library of Congress Cataloging in Publication Data

Hunte, George.
  Barbados.

  Bibliography : p.
  1.   Barbados. I. Title.
F2041.H86   917.29'81'04   73–22383

ISBN 0–8038–0755–4

Contents

List of Illustrations

Acknowledgments

Having been born in Barbados and having lived there from 1917 till 1937, and again from 1948 till 1970, I had exceptional opportunities to study the island's background and to learn directly from hundreds of well-informed Barbadians.

I have read widely and made notes from documents, newspapers and books preserved at the Barbados Museum and Public Library. My searches were partly assisted by the late Eustace Maxwell Shilstone and the late Neville Connell, whose knowledge of Barbadian history was deep rooted.

My own research into the background of Barbadian history was also directed through intensive reading of books by eminent

European and American historians while studying for an honours degree in history at London University.

During the years 1971 and 1972 I read many of the documents relative to Barbados at the Public Records Office in London and made a thorough examination of the excellent collection of notes and manuscripts which the late Darnell Davis bequeathed to the Royal Commonwealth Society.

I wish to thank the librarian and staff of the Royal Commonwealth Society Library, as well as those persons who helped me at both branches of the Public Records Office.

The foreground of the book is my own. It is written from personal experience. Acknowledgments are however due to a number of persons whose advice I found helpful. Among these are Alistair Green of the Barbados Tourist Board, Mrs Genevieve Adams, Jack Dear Q.C., Mrs Rosamond Hunte, and Mr Paul Foster of Paul Foster Travel. Especial thanks are due to my wife Emma who typed the manuscript.

The Author and Publishers would like to thank the following for permission to use photographs in this book: Arts Council of Britain (Pl 4); Barbados Museum (Pl 17); Barbados Tourist Board and Willie Alleyne Associates (Pls 1, 26, 27, 37); Barbados West Indies Tourist Assoc. (Pl 26); Anne Bolt (Pls 19, 20, 21, 23, 28, 29, 34, 35); British Museum (Pls 2, 3, 13, 16); J. Allan Cash (Pls 22 and 32); Metropolitan Museum of Art, New York (Pl 6).

The maps are by courtesy of Patrick Leeson

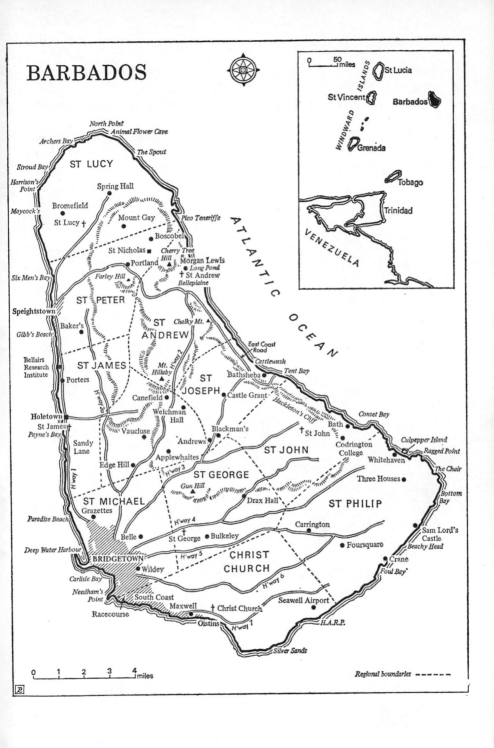

Introduction

The highest praise of Barbados is to be found in *Westward Ho!*, a novel of no great literary merit but representative of English political and commercial attitudes which were prevalent in the decade that preceded the first settlements on the West Indian islands. Through his mother's eyes Charles Kingsley was to see Barbados as 'that lovely isle, the richest gem of all tropic seas.'

Echoing her voice he extolled its wealth, and commerce and beauty and science '. From recollections of the childhood she spent there as the daughter of Nathan Lucas, a rich landowner, Kingsley borrowed splendid images of Barbados at sunrise and sunset. He describes in Homeric language how at dawn 'up flushed the rose, up rushed the sun, whose level rays glittered on the smooth stems of the palm-trees, and threw rainbows across the foam upon the coral reefs and gilded lonely uplands far away', while at sunset the island became 'a long blue bar between the crimson sea and golden sky'.

Kingsley did not exaggerate the natural beauty of Barbados in *Westward Ho!* although he never saw any West Indian islands until 15 years later in 1869. The importance of Barbados in the plot of *Westward Ho!* is magnified by the tradition of its anti-Catholic past. Kingsley, who bitterly resented Newman's defence of his acceptance of Catholicism, selected Barbados as a 'very garden of the Lord' where 'neither Spaniard, cannibal, or evil beast could enter'.

His 'canonisation' of Barbados as a saintly stronghold of the Anglican faith is strange because for almost 200 years the Anglican religion was reserved in Barbados for a minority of people whose lives were spent in a materialistic environment little influenced by piety, and thoroughly debased by the practice of slavery. Yet persistently this legend of the good Anglican and thoroughly English island of Barbados somehow survived and was acknowledged in real, not fictional, terms by James Anthony Froude whose *The English in the West Indies* was written after his visit in 1887.

'England in Barbados', wrote Froude, 'was still a solid fact. The headquarters of the West Indian troops are there. There is a commander-in-chief residing in a "Queen's House" so-called. There is a savannah where there are English barracks under avenues of almond and mahogany. Red coats are scattered about the grass. Officers canter about playing polo, and naval and military uniforms glitter at the side of carriages, and horsemen and horsewomen take their evening rides, as well-mounted and as well-dressed as you can see in Rotten Row.'

Even the language of the 'Anglo-Barbadians was pure English, the voices without the smallest trans-Atlantic intonation'. The parish churches Froude visited were 'solid and respectable' as some still are. Barbados had English police and the English parochial system. It warmed Froude's heart as an Anglican to see St John's church. 'No mass,' he wrote, 'had ever been said at that altar' and he welcomed the sight of 'the old-fashioned seats, the old unadorned communion tables, the old pulpit and reading desk and the clerk's desk below, with the lion and the unicorn conspicuous above the chancel arch'.

Yet despite his lyrical appreciation of Barbados, that 'little England in the tropic seas', Froude was perturbed by doubts and fears about England's future in the island. The sight of palms, stephanotis and jessamine in place of primroses, hyacinths and violets in St John's churchyard made him reflect that ' we too (the English) are perhaps exotics of another kind in these islands, and may not after all have a long abiding place in them.'

Froude's experiences in Barbados were quite unlike those of the prolific English novelist Anthony Trollope who visited Barbados in 1859. His encounters in Barbados were mostly with the Bims, the white Creoles whose smug self-satisfaction irked him considerably.

'The most peculiar distinction' of the Bim, wrote Trollope 'is his voice. There is always a nasal twang about it, but quite distinct from the nasality of the Yankee. The Yankee's word rings sharp through his nose, not so that of the first-class Bim. There is a soft drawl about it and the sound is seldom completely formed. The effect on the ear is the same as that on the hand when a man gives you his to shake, and instead of shaking yours, holds his own still. When a man does so to me I always want to kick him.'

Quickly Trollope adds: 'I had never any wish to kick the Barbadian, more especially as they are all stout men, but I cannot but think that if he were well shaken a more perfect ring would come out of him.'

But the Bims irritated Trollope. He found them as a rule 'larger and fairer' than other West Indian Creoles, but 'less delicate in their limbs and more clumsy in their gait. The male graces are not much studied in Barbados. But it is not only by their form or voice that you may know them—not only by the voice but by the words. No people ever praised themselves so constantly; no set of men were ever so assured that they and their occupations are the main pegs on which the world hangs. Their general law to men would be this: "Thou shalt make sugar in the sweat of thy brow and make it as it is made in Barbados". Any deviation from that law would be a deviation from the high duty of man'.

Yet reluctantly Trollope finds something favourable to say about the island of the Bims. 'It owes no man anything, pays its own way and never makes a poor mouth'. Self-respect, he says, is a fine quality, 'and the Barbadians certainly enjoy that'.

However his parting remarks repeat his disdainful estimate of mimic Barbados. The white Barbadians are parochial, smug people who 'entertain very well' and Barbados, 'is a very respectable little island, and considering the limited extent of its acreage, it does make a great deal of sugar.'

From Trollope derives the embellishment of a story which Dr Pinckard had heard before the nineteenth century opened. 'The story runs,' according to Trollope in *West Indies and the Spanish Main*, 'that when Europe was convulsed by revolutions and wars —when Continental sovereigns were flying hither and thither, and there was so strong a rumour that Napoleon was going to eat us—that then I say the Barbadians sent word over to poor King George the Third, bidding him fear nothing. If England could not protect him, Barbados would.'

Even in loyalty to the throne Trollope found the Barbadians 'self-glorious'. Worse, unlike Froude, who used an umbrella against heat in Bridgetown but found the climate as 'sparkling and invigorating as champagne', Trollope disliked the tropical heat as much as the Bims who gloried in it.

Not so the King's Sergeant Surgeon in 1908, Sir Frederick Treves, who found the climate, 'healthy and agreeable', the air, 'comparatively dry', and the sea-bathing 'cannot be surpassed'.

Was Trollope unfair to Barbados which made him think of the frog that would blow itself out to look as large as an ox? What would he think of Barbados today? We shall never know the answers to either of these questions, but what perennially surprises most people about the island from earliest time to the present is the apparent satisfaction which the people who live there permanently take in their lot. Whatever the reasons, most people in Barbados today are anxious to let it be known to whoever will listen that their way of life is unique and that they are, in the words of the national anthem, 'firm craftsmen' of their fate. That complacency which irked Trollope in the Bims is also prevalent in the new Barbadian of today. Only it is no longer the Bims who lead the chorus. The whole adult population proclaims the Bims' creed as their own.

A disgruntled misanthropist Thomas Walduck wrote of Barbados in 1700:

> O glorious isle in villany excel.
> Sin to the heights, thy fate is Hell.

He accused the people of being a babel of all nations who had blended together and married. The English, he said, had brought with them drunkenness and swearing, the Scotch impudence and falsehood, the Welsh covetousness and revenge, the Irish cruelty and perjury, the Dutch and Danes dissimulation and infidelity.

At the time he wrote the Africans were not regarded as people at all because they were legally real property, otherwise it is possible that he might have attributed to them endurance and cheerfulness.

Certainly a sociologist today in search of a common attribute of Barbadian people would find it hard to define exactly what is their dominant characteristic. In a world of change and rapid communications, transistors, television and films the earth continues to grow smaller minute by minute and the singular qualities

2 and 3 *Lucy, Countess of Carlisle with her husband, James Hay, first Earl of Carlisle*

4 *Captain Thomas Verney, seventeenth-century settler*

5 *Women washing clothes in the river. A painting by Agostino Brunias in the Cunard Gallery, Barbados Museum*

of Barbados are no longer as singular as they were two decades ago. It will be perhaps more rewarding to think of Barbadians as people in motion, people who are in process of fashioning a society in terms of the new situations which have arisen from the fact of independence.

More space has been devoted in the background section to the first hundred years because the events of those years were influenced by the violent upheavals in Europe which preceded the age of absolutism.

The development of Barbados was so intricately intertwined with the development of Europe during those years that its history becomes blurred and confused if it is isolated from the central theatre of Europe. Until the evil of slavery was finally eradicated no modern civilising influences could take root on Barbadian soil.

And when they came these civilising influences had to combat the legacy of two centuries of a class society rooted in the *ancien régime*. The age of reform in Europe had to precede the age of reform in Barbados and in other outposts of Empire.

The Victorian age was an age of progress but it was only towards the end of Victoria's reign that Barbados received the benefits of a reasonable piped water supply. At the same time improved medical facilities and schools made possible the gradual improvements in social life which were foundations for the remarkable progress of the 'fifties and the 'sixties of this century.

The chapters which comprise the Foreground of the book are designed with the principal aim of making it possible for any visitor to Barbados to understand quickly and adequately what the island still has to offer and to offer them the choice of a wide variety of things to do and places to see.

Those who want to explore Barbados thoroughly with the aid of a good road map and a good car will find it profitable to plan their excursions in accordance with the geographical arrangements of the chapters.

7   *Slaves at work and play in the early nineteenth century, from
Waller's A Voyage in the West Indies (1820)*

8   *The comforts a planter might enjoy when bird shooting in
the swamps (Cunard Gallery)*

I BACKGROUND

B

1 Tobacco and Cotton

Sir William Courteen's father went to England as a refugee from the Low Countries in 1568 and prospered there. William, and his brother Peter, were both raised to the order of knighthood by James I to whose privy purse they made handsome contributions. Sir William also made generous contributions to Charles I. From Sir William and another knightly contributor Sir Paul Pindar, King James and his son, Charles, received the enormous amount of £200,000.

Benefits were expected in return for large donations and in that age of privilege and patronage were often given. Sir William had established such a close relationship with James I that the King thought fit to ask him, in a note written from Hampton Court on 30 September 1624, to consider that Richard Fleetwood, Baron of Newton, was a fit match for one of his three daughters. The King went so far as to hope that Sir William would provide this especially favoured daughter with a richer dowry than he intended to give to the other two.

The great merchant prince, Sir William Courteen, who organised the first settlement of Barbados in 1627, had such high standing with James I that he did not hesitate to ask the King for a grant of the 'lands called *Terra Australis Incognita*' in the southern part of the world. As these lands were 'not yet traded to by the King's subjects' he requested a royal grant 'with power to discover the same and plant colonies therein'.

Sir William's request followed conventional English methods of procedure. Between the years 1574 and 1660 no less than 59 charters for settlements were granted by the English Crown. Sir William's request to plant *Terra Australis Incognita* was made in 1625, the year in which one of his captains returning from a trip to South America, where Sir William owned shares in a tobacco plantation, had called at Barbados, the most easterly of the Caribbees, an island not yet inhabited by Europeans.

Sir William noted the advantages to be gained from settling Barbados as a tobacco plantation and may have sought support at this time from the Lord Treasurer, Lord Ley, who was later to become Earl of Marlborough. A note of Lord Ley's dated 1625 recommends Sir William to the King as a 'man who deserved to be respected . . . in regard he so freelie and willinglie lends his money for supplie of His Majesty's occasions and that without interest of the old debt'.

King Charles had succeeded to the throne after the death of his father in March 1625. He did not grant Sir William *Terra Australis Incognita* nor anywhere else. Only a year before another English syndicate formed by a London merchant, Ralph Merrifield and a Suffolk gentleman adventurer, Thomas Warner successfully settled the northern Caribbee island of St. Christopher. Warner had gained experience as a tobacco planter on North's settlement in Guiana. He selected St. Christopher because of its high fertility and for the welcome he had received there from the Carib chief whom he had met on an earlier visit.

In the tight little world of London's merchant traders the success of Warner's foothold upon an island chain which had long been regarded as a Spanish reserve encouraged hopes of a new tobacco boom. The King's Farmer of Customs had reported receipts of nearly £100,000 in 1624 from duties levied on tobacco, which had been imported into England from Virginia, the Somers Islands (Bermuda), Spain and elsewhere. Tobacco was on the lips of every capitalist or fortune hunter who wanted to grow richer in 1625. Planting tobacco on the Caribee islands also appeared as a 'patriotic' duty at a time when English resentment against Spain was being stirred up anew by Buckingham's anti-Spanish policy which followed the failure of the Spanish marriage projected for Prince Charles. Within a month of Charles's succession to the throne in 1625 Attorney-General Heath submitted a memorandum reminding the King of the advantages which the Spanish and Dutch states derived from the West Indies.

The Dutch West Indian Company had been formed in 1621 to encourage Dutch planting in the West Indies and on the mainland of South America and to harry the Spaniards in every way possible, through extension of the conflict they had renewed against Spain in Europe. Dutch aggressiveness in the Caribbean encouraged English designs upon Spanish islands.

Attorney-General Heath advised the young King Charles that it was 'neither safe nor profitable' to have these two European rivals 'absolute lords of these parts'. He urged him to 'openly interfere or permit to be done underhand, and if it prosper make it his own at pleasure.'

In response to a climate of opinion in Court and City circles which was distinctly favourable to tobacco planting, Sir William equipped a ship and selected pioneers to settle Barbados. His first expedition failed to cross the Atlantic in 1626, but in February 1627 Captain Henry Powell brought the *William and John* safely to anchor off the sheltered west coast of Barbados. Eighty English people then went ashore at the place, where the small lagoon in today's Holetown overflows into the sea during high seas and heavy rains. The rowboats which brought the settlers to the golden sands of Barbados were also employed to offload whatever hard rations had survived the long crossing, tools for felling trees and digging the soil, utensils for cooking food, arms and ammunition, personal belongings and motley materials for erecting tents or other temporary shelters against sun and rain. From experience gained on the Courteen plantation at Kijkoveral in Guyana, Powell knew that vegetables would have to be grown quickly on the island if the settlers were to be adequately fed. So he sailed away promptly to visit his friend Groenewegen who was in command of the Guyanese settlement which had been established by Courteen and the Dutchman, Jan de Moor, as long ago as 1616. From Kijkoveral, Henry Powell obtained plant cuttings and vegetable seeds and, most important of all, Arawak men and women who knew how to plant in the tropics and how to prepare foods which were new to the English settlers. Indian corn or maize provided the major ingredient from which lob-lolly (modern cou-cou) was made, cassava produced a bread substitute and sweet potatoes gave additional starch when eaten or a spirituous drink 'mobbie' which might be used as an alternate to water, which had to be obtained from ponds or pools in the gullies or ravines.

The Indian men were expert at fishing with bows and arrows, the shore line teemed with large white land crabs and huge boars rooted in the dense forest. Birds and pigeons also helped to balance the diet.

The settlers had been carefully selected by officers of the Courteen Association and were young enough to undertake the heavy task of felling forest trees and clearing land for planting tobacco and food crops. They also had to build themselves temporary dwelling places in which to sleep. With patience and good fortune the Courteen Association had reason to expect early profits from their adventurous settlement of the most eastern of the Caribbean islands.

But Barbados' distance from the main Caribbean chain of islands did not protect Sir William and his fellow adventurers from the cupidity of noblemen at Charles's Court in London. The Earls of Marlborough and Carlisle, who were both close to the King's person, had realised the possibility of profits to be gained from development of the Caribbees. Already on promise of a fixed annual income from Carlisle the Lord Treasurer Ley had agreed to support the request which Carlisle in 'near attendance upon His Majesty's person' promptly made for all the islands lying between ten and twenty degrees north of the Equator.

A grant of the Caribbees to be known as the Carlisle Province was issued to James the first Earl of Carlisle in the summer of 1627. Barbados and St Christopher were included in the grant despite Courteen's settlement of the first island in February and the commission of 1625 which had made Thomas Warner King's Lieutenant for St Christopher, Nevis, Barbados and Montserrat.

The grant to the Earl of Carlisle was made by Charles I, who acted as King of France, Ireland, Scotland and England. He created and ordained the Earl of Carlisle 'absolute lord of all the Caribbee islands' lying between ten and twenty degrees north latitude.

To justify this very handsome donation Charles explained his motives as arising from a 'laudable and zealous care to increase the Christian religion' and his desire to 'enlarge the territories of his Empire'. The grant records that the Caribbee islands were either 'unknown' or 'in part possessed by certain barbarous men having no knowledge of the Divine Power'.

All of them had appeared on European maps of the world for more than a century while some of them had often been visited by sailors and adventurers during the reigns of Elizabeth and

James the First. Nonetheless, and despite the most recent settlement made by the Warner and Courteen syndicates, Charles' grant gave the Earl of Carlisle exclusive credit for 'discovery of the Caribbees' and for having 'at his great cost and charge' brought them to the pass of 'a large and copious colony of English'.

Such was the courtly language and the methods of monarchs when they disposed of properties which they did not own to lords whom they especially favoured. Charles, King, 'by the grace of God' gave all the Caribbee islands to a man who had been a great favourite of his father and who was at this time one of his own faithful Privy Councillors and an experienced diplomat.

Warner considered it tactful to accept Carlisle's lordship over St Christopher, Nevis and his two other islands of Barbuda and Montserrat. In Barbados, however, Courteen's settlers were unlikely to let the Earl of Carlisle enjoy revenue from plantations which they were still then clearing of trees. On Barbados trees grew so thickly down to the water's edge that they justified the name, 'the bearded islands', which Portuguese sailors had given to the island and the small satellite-islet which lay south of the Hole near the entrance to the small harbour where Bridgetown was soon to be built. This island, called Pelican after the bird which nested there, remained until 1960 when it was swallowed up by the modern deep water harbour.

Sir William knew that a man in Carlisle's style of life needed much income from the Caribbees to pay off his most urgent creditors. Court circles in London had never forgotten the feast which Carlisle, when he was still Viscount Doncaster, had given to the French Ambassador in 1621. For that occasion 100 cooks had worked for eight days to cook 1600 dishes.

Carlisle was only one of many great spenders. (The painter-diplomat Paul Rubens, reporting to his master Olivares in 1629 recorded the sumptuous living of all the leading nobles at Charles's Court, observing how they spent 'money lavishly so that the majority of them are hopelessly in debt'.)

Sir William feared for his dividends if Carlisle were to get full control of Barbados. So he took prompt action and persuaded another old favourite of James I, Philip Herbert, Earl of Montgomery to beg of Charles I a grant of the Montgomery Province in which Barbados was made to appear as though it were not one of the Caribbee islands. Philip Herbert, who was soon to become the 4th Earl of Pembroke, had been Lord Chamberlain since 1626 and was well known to Courteen as an investor in overseas enterprises. He had been associated with the Virginia and East India companies and with a company trading to Guiana. He quickly saw the opportunities to be gained from Barbados and manoeuvred to have it included with Trinidad and Tobago in a grant which made no mention of the Caribbees. Barbados and Fonseca (a name which possibly could have been used by sailors to describe Pelican Island) were both included with Trinidad and Tobago and granted to Philip Earl of Montgomery in February 1628. The draughtsman duly recorded that the islands of the Montgomery Province lay between 8 and 13 degrees north latitude and had been acquired by the Earl at 'great expense with the good intention to transport thither a colony of English'. The Earl of Montgomery was one of Charles's favourite hunting companions and he had doubtless also been duly rewarded by Courteen for championing his claims to Barbados.

Neither Montgomery nor Courteen seem to have given much attention to the obvious fact that Montgomery's province encroached upon the Caribbees, which had been defined as lying between ten and twenty degrees north latitude. Barbados at 13 degrees north was located within Carlisle's province of all the Caribbees.

Was Courteen buying time through Pembroke's intervention? Hindsight suggests he was.

The London merchant syndicate to whom Carlisle had already awarded 10,000 acres of the virgin soil of Barbados in return for advances of money were not slow to anticipate the difficulties which might arise from a clash over proprietorship between two Court favourites. They quickly persuaded the Earl of Carlisle to ask for a second grant of the Caribbees in which his rights to Barbados were spelt out specifically. The grant was issued in April 1628 and Barbados was identified as 'Barbudas alias Barbades, alias Barbudos, alias Barbadus'. To avoid any confusion with Barbuda, which had been one of the four islands named in Warner's commission, that island was described in Carlisle's new grant as 'Barbido' and 'Barbudo'.

When the King later sought to justify his 'double-grant' of

Barbados to each of his father's two former favourites he blamed
the mistake as having 'arisen chiefly in the ambiguity of names of
near sound . . . subject to mistaking in so remote parts'. A king
can do no wrong, but the explanation rings thin on modern
ears.

The King was at the time commenting on the verdict which
had been handed down by Lord Keeper Coventry in April 1629
in favour of the Earl of Carlisle's rights to Barbados. In a letter
to Carlisle's governor, Charles Wolverston, he upheld that verdict,
saying that ' Lord Carlisle's title to Barbados is declared to be of
full strength and none other is to have force'.

Wolverston had served in Bermuda and had been recommended
to Carlisle as the person most suitable to be in charge of the
delicate office of governing two separate plantation syndicates,
both engaged in breaking up and planting the forest lands of
Barbados. Wolverston had a special recommendation for Carlisle
in that he had known Courteen's deputy governor William Deane
in Bermuda. Through Deane's introduction Wolverston was able
to present Carlisle's friendly letter to John Powell, Courteen's
governor. Soon after he landed in midsummer 1628 with some 80
settlers selected by the Syndicate of London merchants,
Wolverston presented the letter in which the Earl invited Powell
and Deane to welcome the new arrivals as 'friends and countrymen, the addition of whose strength but further your securities,
without any way impeaching your profit'. It was a sensible plea
for peaceful co-existence amongst Englishmen whose presence
in Barbados could be challenged at any time by French and
Spanish men of war, since England was then fighting France
and Spain.

Wolverston's settlers had avoided the sheltered West Coast of
Barbados where Courteen's men had come ashore, and had
instead entered the natural harbour at the point where the sea
merged with the water from a small river. They came ashore by
means of an old bridge which they believed had been built by
Indians. Whether it had been or not this bridge gave rise to the
name of 'Indian Bridge' which was the first title of the city which
later came to be called Bridgetown.

Having established his bridgehead and having found that his
friend Deane was willing to acknowledge his right to represent

the interests of Carlisle, Wolverston next took steps to obtain authority over the whole island. With Deane's help he easily persuaded some of Courteen's settlers that they would gain more from supporting Carlisle's interest in Barbados because they would be getting outright grants of land instead of shares in the crops which were growing on lands belonging to the Courteen Association. By such powerful bribes Wolverston seduced the loyalty of a majority of Courteen's settlers, who now exceeded 600 persons, and proclaimed Carlisle's commission which had been given to him as governor of the whole island of Barbados.

Courteen regarded Wolverston's claim to be governor of the whole of Barbados as a threat to the rights he claimed by reason of the grant made to the Earl of Montgomery. Unwisely, he did not await the legal settlement of the dispute between the two earls but sent out his senior partner Henry Powell to restore his authority in Barbados by force. Henry successfully reinstated John Powell as governor and sailed back to England with a cargo of tobacco. He also took with him as prisoners Charles Wolverston and William Deane.

Lord Coventry's judgement in favour of Carlisle completely nullified, Courteen's claim to Barbados, which had only existed by reason of the inclusion of Barbados in the grant made by Charles to the Earl of Montgomery.

Far from making a profit on a troublesome venture which had taken four years to plan and implement and which had cost about £10,000 Courteen made a total loss. He and his partners had taken all the risks and had been the pioneer promoters of a settlement which endured, but Courteen had neglected to do the one thing needful for his success: he did not obtain a Royal grant confirming his right to act as he had done. Carlisle reaped where Courteen had sowed, but Carlisle took pains to obtain the early Royal sanction which Courteen had sought too late. Some historians have seen in Courteen's petition for a grant of *Terra Australis Incognita* an attempt by Courteen to get control of the Caribbees, but this seems unlikely in view of Courteen's normal business methods. The policy of the Courteen Association was always to act first, negotiate afterwards. Courteen had settled Barbados long before Buckingham's assassination in August 1628. He may have hoped that Buckingham would support his initiative because he was known to be a generous contributor to the Royal privy purse.

After Buckingham's death a new situation arose as Charles I avoided reliance on any single favourite and sought majority approval for his acts from the Privy Council.

Courteen's attempt to win the Lord Chamberlain's support was typical of a man who was willing to try anything once. He was unlikely to succeed against the greater batteries of influence which Carlisle could command, not least that of his beautiful wife Lucy, one of the mosty witty and influential ladies at Court and an intimate friend of Queen Henrietta Maria.

Barbados in the early years of settlement was a dismal place to live and far removed from the splendours and civilisation of Charles's Court. Some of the young men who had left England in search of fortunes had quickly become disillusioned by the continuing intrigues of their feudal overlords and had grown weary of the hardships and inconvenience of their daily battle against tropical Nature. They took to roving from island to island, some reaching as far north as Bermuda and the colonies established on the east coast of North America. Others took to privateering, or returned to England.

The exodus from Barbados was encouraged by the despotic regime which the London merchants soon encouraged Carlisle to establish there. The Earl's first choice to succeed Charles Wolverston as governor was Sir William Tufton, a younger brother of the Earl of Thanet.

Sir William thought his duty was to establish a society of gentlemen in Barbados. To this end he organised six vestry administrations to look after the needs of the settlers along the coastline and the interior nearer to Bridgetown. He enacted local laws which were passed with the consent of a council representative of the leading settlers.

His attempt to create a society of overseas English gentlemen on the lines of the New England colonies was not approved by the London merchants who had been commissioned by Carlisle. They regarded Barbados exclusively as a plantation to be worked and which had to grow and produce tobacco in large enough quantities to repay them for the monies they had supplied to the Earl of Carlisle. They also wished to make profits from their investments. They were able to persuade the Earl, who had hopes of gain from his private plantations in Barbados as well as from the duties which he was empowered to impose and retain to his own use for a period of ten years, to withdraw Tufton's commission and give it to a man who understood exactly what was wanted in Barbados.

Carlisle, whose ear was always open to schemes of greater profit making, was easily persuaded, so Henry Hawley, the violent young Captain who had forcibly ejected Courteen's governor John Powell from Barbados in 1629, was sent out to Barbados to rule as Carlisle's third governor.

Barbados for the next ten years was moulded in Hawley's image. Hawley was a man of iron living in an age of iron. When Sir Thomas Tufton attempted to rally those gentlemen who regarded themselves as gentlemen settlers and who still hoped to create a society in Barbados Hawley accused him of disloyalty, rigged a court martial which found him guilty of treason and had him shot and his chief supporters hanged. From Hawley's point of view he had done the right thing. Men who wanted to establish a society of honourable gentlefolk tilling the soil and producing food for themselves and crops for export were pursuing their own private interests. Barbados had not been settled for such reasons, as Hawley and his employers saw it.

The planting of tobacco and the yields of any other suitable crop were intended to benefit merchants in London, not settlers in Barbados. The settlers had been selected to make profits for the syndicate in London.

Hawley's methods of administration were directed exclusively to maintaining his position as governor by producing maximum returns for those who employed him. At the same time he lost no opportunity to acquire plantations for himself in order to ensure direct benefits from the work he was doing for Carlisle and the London merchants.

Taxes were levied by Hawley on every man, woman or child who was resident on a plantation. Those who did not pay 40 pounds weight of tobacco or cotton for each resident were put in prison. Taxes were collected even from persons who 'killed pigeons, sold beer or kept storehouses'. Discipline in Barbados was maintained through martial law, hanging, flogging, cropping of ears, branding and merciless fines. Ministers of religion were treated as 'mercenaries' and forced to do the governor's bidding.

A harsh regime devoted only to profit making, in a place where 'ignorance both of the laws of God and man doth domineer' is the judgment on Barbados made by a visiting Anglican priest, the Reverend Thomas Lane in 1637. The comment might with justice have been made of many less favoured places than Barbados that year, but it should dispel any lingering fancies which may be entertained by persons who are prone in every age to believe that the days of old, in a world now lost, were golden days!

The decade which followed the settlement of Barbados was a miserable period for all but a few whose fortunes prospered. Sir Henry Colt, who visited Barbados in 1631 and described Governor Hawley as a young man 'naturally inclined to modesty and temperance', felt very sorry for the Englishmen he met there. They were all young men of good descent, he wrote in a letter to his son George, but their chief fault was 'excessive drinking'. They knew very little about farming and kept their servants too idle. Their grounds and plantations showed what they were: 'all are bushes and long grass . . . soil nothing but loose sand, half a foot deep, and there will be found nothing but clay . . . their water thick and not of the best . . . rivers . . . no other than little pits . . . as for their houses they are so distant one from the other they could not unite any strong force to resist invaders'.

No modern public relations firm given such dismal facts would want to produce a brochure in favour of tobacco planting in Barbados! Yet the true position was even worse than Sir Henry had described it to his son. For in that very year of 1631 a decree had gone forth to the Lord Proprietor of all the Caribbees from the Privy Council ordering him to limit tobacco planting in all places under his command. Furthermore, a warning was given that only 'sweet, wholesome and well-packed tobacco should be exported, and to the port of London only'. This early warning note of English governmental interference in colonial affairs was to grow stronger till by 1634 it produced a commission headed by Archbishop Laud with powers amongst others to 'remove Governors and require an account of their government: to appoint judges as magistrates and establish courts; to hear and determine all manners of complaints for the colonies: to have

power over all charters and patents, and to revoke those sur-
reptitiously obtained'. Conditions in England which were then
leading up to the Civil War made the implementation of such
a policy quite impossible. The possibility of a drastic over-
haul of the fiefdom of Carlisle would not therefore have disturbed the London merchants unduly. Their immediate anxiety
was to find a substitute for tobacco as a major export. They
turned to cotton.

In 1639 the Knight Martial of the King's Household received a
letter addressed to him at the piazza, Covent Garden. In it his
son Tom, an adventurous young man who had tried Virginia and
Europe before going out to Barbados, promises 'by the grace of
God' to send him 'as much cotton home as will countervayle twice
the summe of money' he should have lent him. A year later Tom
describes in detail the needs of a Barbadian farmer before cotton,
following tobacco, gave place to King Sugar as the major pro-
ducer of wealth in Barbados.

He wanted 20 able men-servants, of whom two must be joiners
and two sawyers. They are required to bring their tools with them.
In addition he needed stores and clothes for his workers: 12
dozen drawers, shirts and shoes, 4 dozen Monmouth capes, 4
dozen coarse neckcloths, 2 dozen broadhose, 2 dozen narrow
hose, 6 spades, 6 shovels, 6 pick axes, 2 great iron kettles (one 10
gallon, one 8 gallon), 2 great iron pots (one 8 gallon, one 6 gallon), one 4 gallon pot, one stew pot, 20 coarse bed tick hammocks,
10 bolts of packing canvas, 10,000 sixpenny nails, 5000 tenpenny
nails, 5000 hobnails, some twine, whited brown thread, pack
needles and sewing needles.

The list indicates how dependent the farmers of cotton were
upon their own servants to package their crops for export and
how simple were the arrangements made to accommodate, clothe
and feed them.

Tom naturally desired less austere items of clothing for himself.
His father was invited to send him 6 shorts, 12 pairs of linen boot
hose, 2 pairs of 'long enough' boots, 6 pairs of the long elevenses
('for I am fain to wear them a size longer here than in England,
because we travel so much a foot in the island'), one stuff suit,
one dimity suit.

Finally Tom plucked up all his courage and requested one com-

modity that 'never lyeth upon merchants' hands in this island:
which is drink'.

He offers to dispose of over 50 cases of good spirit for his
father's profit. 'I make no question,' he writes, 'but you will have
great gaynes from them . . . they are generally such great drunk-
ards in this island that they will find coppers to buy their drinks
although they go without themselves. Such is their lewdness and
their ill qualities in this and all other islands.'

Tom Verney had gone to Barbados bearing a letter of introduction from the Earl of Warwick to Governor Hawley, who had
obtained for him a plantation of 100 acres. Tom's affairs did not
prosper and he had to be bailed out of a Bridgetown gaol for debt
by a certain Richard Gregory whose house in Barbados was appro-
priately called 'Laus Deo'. Debts were constant swords of
Damocles hanging over the heads of young planters in Barbados
during the early years of settlement.

Labour shortage also added to their afflictions. In 1642, before
returning to England to fight for Charles I, Tom Verney in a letter
informed his father that his cotton had been shipped in a Dutch
vessel bound for Amsterdam and begged him to find out whether
'it were possible for me and your men, with the great help
of Bridewell and prisons to procure in two months space an
hundred men or more, which if they are to be got I shall be
mighty joyfull'.

Failure to obtain workers from England was a contributing
factor to the development of a trade in slaves from Africa to
Barbados and other plantations in the Caribbees.

Thomas Verney had arrived in Barbados after Hawley had
changed his allegiance to the Earl of Warwick. The Earl of Carlisle had died in 1636 and Hawley had been retained as governor
by the second Earl and his fellow trustees of Carlisle's estates.
From a report by Sir Thomas Warner, who had been knighted
and made sole Governor for life of St Christopher in 1629, it
seems that Hawley began to have differences with his employers
in London as early as 1636. According to Sir Thomas a scheme to
settle Martinique, one of the Caribbee islands granted to the first
Earl, had failed because of Hawley's refusal to co-operate.

Sir Thomas had despatched his son-in-law to Barbados to ask
Hawley permission to recruit 500 men equipped with arms and

rations to strengthen his assault forces against Martinique. Hawley had behaved in a manner which Sir Thomas described to Secretary Windebank as 'obstinate and rebellious'. In view of the shortage of labour and the fact that Barbados in 1636 had no more than 6000 English residents, Hawley may have been justified in thinking that the loss of 500 men would be detrimental to the Barbadian economy. Sir Thomas's complaint undoubtedly damaged Hawley's reputation with his employers, who felt that the time had come for more vigorous efforts to settle plantations on other Caribbee islands before strangers moved in.

Disagreement between the trustees and Carlisle as to their jurisdiction over the Caribbees probably encouraged the Earl of Warwick to make a bid for Barbados through acquisition of the Earl of Pembroke's rights to the Montgomery Province. Warwick found an accomplice in Hawley, who promised to win over the chief planters in Barbados and to provide settlers for Tobago and Trinidad.

The second Earl of Carlisle, getting wind of Warwick's intentions, dismissed Hawley and appointed Sergeant Major Henry Huncks to replace him as governor of Barbados. The King confirmed the appointment and sent an instruction to the governor, council, planters and inhabitants of the Caribbee Isles, requesting them to do their uttermost to oppose any who may attempt to 'allure' the inhabitants from those islands 'whereby the Earl will be disabled of sufficient people to plant the residue'.

Hawley's decision to support Warwick, whose star was now rising in England as a leading member of the Puritan rebels who were getting ready to abolish conciliar and prerogative government, was doubtless influenced by his jealousy and resentment of Sir Thomas Warner, who had been created Lieutenant General of the Caribbees, in addition to his life governorship of St Christopher. Hawley planned his moves with care. On a visit to England he obtained a roving commission from the King to visit English tobacco plantations overseas and to discuss with their governors proposals for limitations of output and price controls. Then, hurrying back to Barbados before Carlisle's new governor could arrive in 1639, he used this new warrant which had been issued to him as Lieutenant General and Governor of Barbados as authority for establishing a republican régime which was similar

9 *and* 10 *(opposite) Bridgetown early this century. Above: Trafalgar Square. Below: Broad Street*

in concept to those operating in the Puritan colonies of Massachusetts and Providence.

Henry Huncks later reported to the Earl of Carlisle upon Hawley's illegal acts. Hawley, he said, had got to Barbados before him, called in all commissions, proclaimed all offices void, made the gaol delivery a day of mercy, chose burgesses and settled a parliament. He refused to let Huncks read his commission, ordered him to give it up on threat of arrest, and disputed Carlisle's proprietorship of the island. Hawley's 'parliament' then chose Hawley as governor and proclaimed him 'with the greatest scorn' to Carlisle. Unable to take over as Carlisle's governor in Barbados, Huncks sailed off to Antigua to await instructions from England.

Hawley's high-handed actions were duly investigated; a commission of inquiry found that his 'liberal distribution of power was the cloud between the eyes of the people and the clearness of the King's intentions'. Huncks was recalled from Antigua, Hawley's property in Barbados was sequestrated and he was sent over to England in charge of John Hanmer, one of the commissioners. In England Hawley's friends in high places were soon active on his behalf and by January 1641 an order of the Privy Council ordered the governor of Barbados to see that Hawley's estates in Barbados were restored to him and commanded the Earl of Carlisle and the feoffees of the late Earl to make good whatever losses Hawley had sustained through sequestration

The changing political situation in England before the outbreak of fighting between Parliament and the King may have been responsible for the seesaw of influences which the Earl of Carlisle and the Earl of Warwick were exercising with regard to Barbados. Tom Verney in 1639 had referred to the 'Earl of Warwick's buying Barbados' in a letter to his father, while Philip Burlamachi in the same year reported to Secretary Windebank his belief that King Charles had favourably noticed his 'request concerning the Earl of Carlisle, who he understands had made an agreement with the Earl of Warwick for the possession of the Barbados islands.' Some *rapprochement* between Warwick and Carlisle seems to have taken place, for Carlisle's next appointment of governor to succeed Henry Huncks in 1641 was Philip Bell, a former governor of Bermuda and the man whom Warwick had selected to govern the Providence islands on behalf of the Puritan Adventurers. Bell

11 *(opposite) Stone drawing of Nelson's Statue, Bridgetown in 1847*

was also married to the daughter of Warwick's old privateering associate in Bermuda, Daniel Elfrith.

Bell arrived in Barbados during the year 1641, after leading an unsuccessful expedition to St Lucia in 1640 in support of a settlement which had been started there by Sir Thomas Warner. He was appointed governor's deputy in 1642 and later in 1645 was commissioned as governor during Warwick's régime as Governor in chief of all the Plantations in America. Although Warwick's own high appointment had not been made until 1643, his influence in Barbados was already great enough in 1642 to obtain a supply of men to go with his liegeman Captain Marshall to attempt a settlement in Tobago. It is probable that Bell assisted Warwick in securing men for this expedition and he also most likely helped Captain Jackson to obtain 650 men from Barbados to join the anti-Spanish crusade in the Indies which had been financed by Warwick and other members of the Providence company in retaliation against the sack and destruction of their colony by the Spaniards in 1641.

Bell's position in Barbados before 1643 reflected the uncertainties which existed because of Warwick's claims to all of the islands named in the grant of the Montgomery Province. In that year Warwick's star reached its highest point when Oliver Cromwell, Pym, the Earl of Pembroke and Montgomery and other Parliamentary Commissioners for Plantations, named him Governor in Chief of all the Plantations in America. In the same year Parliament through confiscation of the estates of the second Earl of Carlisle, who had taken the King's side in the Civil War, automatically relieved the English settlers in the Caribbees from the burden of proprietary dues. Both Bell and Warner overnight thereby became servants of the Earl of Warwick, Parliament's Controller for all overseas plantations.

What happened in Barbados or what happened in any other English plantation overseas was now to be dictated by the course of war in England. It turned out that Parliament and Warwick had to leave the plantations to fend for themselves until victory was secured. It was Bell's chance to rule as he wanted. He took it and set Barbados on a course which was to make it known as the richest gem of the English crown.

2 Sugar, Rebellion and Empire

The nineteenth-century historian of Barbados, John Poyer, described Bell as the Barbadian Justinian for the number of laws passed during his régime, and comments that Barbadians then began to enjoy the benefits of equal laws and social order. Ligon on the other hand visited Barbados in 1647 to find only a few of the early planters still living on the island. He describes the bustling activity of a harbour with 22 ships riding at anchor, despite the ravages of plague which soon got out of hand, 'the living' being 'hardly able to bury the dead'. The island was temporarily short of food. Ligon's estimate of a resident population of not less than 50,000 souls, besides negroes, has been considered very high, especially as another estimate made for the year 1645 put the English at only 23,980 persons.

Slave trading was not far advanced in 1647. Ligon noted that slaves and their posterity were 'kept and preserved with greater care than the servants' whose status as property of their masters ended after 5 years' continuous labour. Ligon saw such cruelty done to servants as he did not 'think one Christian could have done to another'. So cruel was the treatment that shortly before Ligon's arrival the majority of servants appointed a day to fall upon their masters and cut all their throats, thereby making themselves 'free men and masters of the island'. The plot was discovered and 18 ringleaders were put to death.

Ligon gave three reasons why negro slaves who were 'more than double the numbers of the Christians' did not plot rebellions. Firstly they were not allowed to touch weapons, secondly they were low-spirited, thirdly they spoke different tongues as they came from different parts of Africa.

Amongst the masters Ligon found some who had raised themselves to high estate, others in a 'declining and yielding condition'. Some were so poorly housed that their little low-roofed rooms were 'like stoves or heated ovens'. More prosperous planters built their homes like fortifications with 'lines, bulwarks and bastions to defend themselves'. The accepted warning signal for disorders or tumults amongst rebellious servants or slaves was a musket discharge, sounded in turn from house to house, throughout the occupied part of the island.

Plantations had in the first decade of settlement been located chiefly along west and south coastal strips. When Ligon arrived intensive forest clearance of Barbados had started, but the interior of the island and most of the East Coast was still standing-timber land. The spurt given to sugar production in the Caribbees after the Dutch were driven out of Brazil in 1654 intensified the rate of forest clearance on Barbados: by 1655 the landscape had taken on the appearance of large treeless plantations of sugar cane. A report of 1671 notes that 'at the Barbadoes all the trees are destroyed, so that wanting wood to boyle their sugar, they are forced to send for coales from England'.

Large supplies of timber for fuel helped to persuade planters who were searching for more profitable crops than tobacco or cotton to choose sugar cane. The changeover, however, was gradual. Ligon describes a large plantation in 1647. Of its 500 acres, 200 were planted in cane, 120 were woodland, 70 were allotted to household crops, 30 were under tobacco, and the remainder were growing cotton, ginger and fruit trees.

Ligon was favourably impressed by most planters, whom he describes as men of great abilities and parts. They needed to be because of the work required of them if their plantations were to become productive and prosperous. Regular weeding of the fields, and planting required personal supervision unless a truly able overseer could be found. The Ingenio or sugar works was a complex of boiling house, coppers and furnaces, filling rooms, still house and curing house. Much could go wrong during manufacture of sugar if maintenance in the Ingenio was either slovenly or neglected. Cattle and horses could die of disease or be poisoned if they ate harmful grasses. A regular supply of working animals such as cattle, horses, asses, and camels was subject to ordinary mercantile risks which at the time included piracy as well as shipwreck and fire. Industry, anticipation, fortitude were ingredients for success in the 'sweet negotiation of sugar' which had already by the time of Ligon's departure in 1650 brought some planters to great fortune. Colonel James Drax, for instance, had begun planting in Barbados with a capital of only £300, but was so enriched by sugar cane cultivation that his thoughts had turned towards acquisition of an English estate which would yield £10,000 yearly. Colonel Modyford, who had been a fellow traveller with Ligon in 1647, looked to gain £100,000 from his Barbadian plantation before he thought of going back to England.

It was during the troublous years when men of property were striving in England to control King or Parliament, that other Englishmen were striving for riches in Barbados. To succeed in sugar production much capital investment was needed. Ligon's estimate was £14,000, a very large sum for those days.

England's difficulties provided opportunities for Dutch entrepreneurs to instruct the English who were planting in Barbados how to grow canes and how to convert the juice from the ripe canes into molasses, syrup, sugar and the liquor kill-devil or rumbullion. They were able too to supply all necessary machinery and the fast ships which were required for a two-way trade between the island and Europe. At the same time they were able to transport Africans from their trading stations across the Atlantic to augment the labour force which was urgently needed to clear large areas of timberland and plough them up for sugar cane planting. Dutch ships and others built in New England were almost the only ones available for bringing in cattle, horses, foodstuffs and other imports which the English obtained in exchange for their exports of cotton, indigo, ginger, tobacco, sugar and fustic wood. The early contact between settlers in the Caribbee islands and the mainland colonies was later to strengthen the economies of both and continued unbroken until the American Revolution shattered this trading pattern.

In the early years of sugar expansion from the mid-forties of the sixteenth century Dutch ships formed the majority of the estimated 100 which Ligon said called at Barbados yearly. They brought essential tools, material and equipment required by carpenters, joiners, smiths, masons, mill-wrights, wheel-wrights, tinkers and coopers, the men whose specialist skills were indispensable for the manufacture and export of sugar.

If there was a time prior to November 1966 when the island of Barbados looked after its own commercial interests without overseas intervention it was during the years 1643 to 1651 when outside control from England was impossible because of the Civil War and its consequences. Those were golden years for Dutch capitalists and English planters when the virgin soils of Barbados yielded rich crops of sugar cane.

It would be a mistake, however, to suppose that the English in Barbados during these years of profit-making untrammelled by proprietors' dues sought political independence of any kind. Those men who advised the governor in council or assembly for the most part were anxious only to obtain profits which would enable them to return to England when the war was over and become men of property and status there. Their political attitudes followed mainly the lines which were developing in England in those troubled years. Many modern historians now accept the view that support for the King in the higher echelons of society during the Civil War came from the nobility and gentry, while commercial and industrial interests were mostly on the side of Parliament. So neat a contrast of opposed interests was hardly to be found in England, but in Barbados it was irrelevant to local conditions. Englishmen in Barbados maintained the political attitudes they had adopted while living in England, but then the issues at stake in England had not been exported to Barbados. It was not until the later years of the first Civil War, when a fairly large number of extreme Royalist supporters fled to Barbados, that serious consideration began to be given by them to making the island a stronghold for the Stuart monarchy. Barbados, unlike St Christopher, which had to tolerate French settlers from the beginning, was exclusively occupied by English settlers and was the most flourishing of the properties in the Carlisle Province.

In 1647 the second Earl had constituted Francis, Lord Willoughby of Parham as Lieutenant General of all the Caribbee islands, thinking that he would be able to use his influence with Parliament to secure incomes for them both. Willoughby's commission was to last 21 years and was dated from Michaelmas 1646.

Carlisle had turned to Willoughby for assistance when he was still influential in Parliamentary circles. The House of Lords had in 1645 restored his rights to the Carlisle Province on payment of a fine of £800, in recompense for having taken the side of King Charles I. Carlisle's action followed the lines of a general practice adopted by many Royalists, who often recovered their sequestrated lands by re-purchasing through intermediaries. Wealth during the Civil War did not pass from old nobility to new landed gentry.

Willoughby's patent had been issued by Carlisle in the year that the army obtained real power in England. Because he resisted their proposals for reform in the House of Lords, when Speaker, Willoughby was impeached and imprisoned in the Tower. He later escaped to Holland, where he declared himself a supporter of Charles II.

It is likely that the renewal of Carlisle's proprietary rights caused Bell and his advisers in Barbados to refuse both the overtures which had been made by Charles I in 1645 and later by Parliament in 1646 to assert their respective authorities over Barbados. His policy of neutrality, which indirectly helped the growth and prosperity of the planters, also encouraged the new Royalists who began to flock to Barbados after the Army in England had purged the Long Parliament in December 1648 and initiated the rule of 'the Rump'. Once these men had decided to try the King and Cromwell had made up his mind to cut off Charles' head 'with the Crown upon it', a policy of toleration between King's supporters and Parliament's supporters was no longer possible anywhere for Englishmen. When the axe fell on 30 January 1649 the moment of truth had arrived!

When that tragic news reached Barbados weeks later even the sugar growers dedicated to fortune-seeking had to stand up and be counted for or against the Stuarts.

Nicholas Foster was one who chose the republican side, although he had supported the neutralist policy which had been favoured by Governor Bell. Englishmen in Barbados, he wrote after his banishment from the island in 1650, were at peace during all the time of England's troubles, living in great content with each other. But towards the latter end of the wars divers Cavaliers came over 'pretending to have done great service for His Majesty'. Obtaining seats on the Governor's councils they began to act in a very high nature, 'cutting out tongues, stigmatising and banishing all such persons as they had anything against'. Foster described a Royalist *coup d'état* as a horrid rebellion, but the Royalists who engineered it could, with justice, see themselves as liberators of an island whose legitimate sovereign had been executed by men who held republican views and whose frightful suppression of Irish and Scots by means of General Oliver Cromwell had made their behaviour in Barbados seem mild by comparison.

It is interesting to note that Ligon, whose humanitarian feelings made him an early advocate of christening slaves, regarded Colonel Walrond, the Royalist 'rebel' leader in Barbados, as a man full of good works, who got 'such love of his servants as they thought all too little they could do for him'. He described Walrond as one of 'the discreeter and better natured men' who had come to rule in Barbados toward the end of the Civil War.

Because of the success of the Royalists in controlling the governor in council and as elected members of the assembly, on 3 May 1650 Charles II was proclaimed in Barbados as 'King of England, Scotland, France, Ireland, Barbados and all other plantations'. Then, as now, the English sovereign commanded the loyalties of Englishmen no matter where they resided.

Royalist supremacy in Barbados had been largely achieved by Colonel Walrond and his brother, both men of Devon. They made it relatively easy for Lord Willoughby some days later to proclaim his commission as Lieutenant Governor of the Caribbees under Carlisle's patent which Charles II had endorsed in Holland. Leaving the Walronds to administer Barbados, Willoughby left on a visit of familiarisation to the neighbouring islands of his province. Unlike the two Earls of Carlisle, Willoughby took a keen personal interest in promoting the advancement of the Caribbee islands. He was also under the obligation to remit half of the provincial revenues to Carlisle for payment of his father's debts. After the execution of Charles I and the establishment of the Rump oligarchy it was vital for him to go to Barbados to defend his property from attack by the new rulers of England.

All the English plantations had been given notice of the change of government in England and their inhabitants were required to continue their obedience 'as they looked for protection'. Willoughby recognised in this proclamation a bid by the London merchants who were close to the Rump oligarchy to achieve a monopoly for themselves in the Caribbees. He realised that Bell would have to change his policy of neutrality and make an effort to persuade the English in Barbados to accept the new power structure which had been established in their country of birth. Bell easily persuaded the assembly to pass an act for 'uniting the inhabitants of the island by means of an oath not to oppose the civil government', but the Royalist *coup d'état* frustrated his intentions.

When Willoughby returned to Barbados the republicans, who included Nicholas Foster, Colonel Drax, Colonel Alleyne and about 100 more prosperous planters, had already been banished to England by the Walrond brothers whom he had appointed to keep order during his absence. Bell meanwhile retired to live in St Christopher.

In England the republican planters exerted pressure upon the small Committee for Trade and Plantations who then exercised power on behalf of the Rump Parliament's Council of State. They were helped a great deal by Oliver Cromwell and the Earl of Warwick who had not given up his ambitions for taking over Barbados and other islands. Trade with Barbados was forbidden and a decision taken to send a fleet of warships under command of Sir George Ayscue to subdue Barbados, Bermuda, Antigua, Virginia and Maryland and force them to renounce Charles II as their sovereign lord.

Anticipating these measures of the Rump Parliament Willoughby put Barbados on a war footing. He sequestrated the properties of banished planters and imposed monthly contributions of sugar from others. Fortifications were strengthened to defend the island from attack by sea, and a very large shipment of sugar was sent over to Holland to pay for armaments which were needed for his army of about 600 fighting men. Servants were conscripted and drilled in companies. By emphasising the necessity of trade with Holland as the only credible method of maintaining the prosperity of the sugar trade Willoughby convinced the men of property in Barbados that their only hope for the future lay in defiance of the power-seekers who had 'temporarily' got control in England. Finally he rallied the hopes of newly arrived Royalists by issuing an invitation to Prince Rupert to come to Barbados and make it a major base for attacks upon King Charles II's enemies everywhere.

Meanwhile his enemies in England had realised that if Willoughby were to succeed in Barbados the other rebellious plantations might combine to fight the Civil War overseas. So the warrant issued to Sir George Ayscue on 1 February 1651 instructed him 'to reduce Barbados to the obedience of the Commonwealth'. To achieve this goal he was authorised to 'force the inhabitants to submission, to land men, surprise their forts, beat down their castles and places of strength, and to seize all ships and vessels belonging to them or any others trading there'.

To safeguard the property of the Republicans in Barbados two other Commissioners were sent along with Ayscue, who had to obtain their approval before launching offensives upon the plantations in Barbados.

Seven months passed before Ayscue's seven ships sighted Carlisle Bay in Barbados. Willoughby had in the meanwhile published his war aims. In June he and the Council and Assembly of Barbados declared their firm resolution 'never to permit His Majesty's undoubted right to Barbados to be questioned' and accused the English Council of State of planning to 'force a Governor upon them and a garrison of 1200 men to be maintained by the island, as well as renounce their allegiance to the King.'

Willoughby's determination to resist the men of the Rump Parliament is easily understood. The decisive battle of Worcester had not yet taken place in England and the numbers of Royalists in Barbados exceeded by at least 5000 the forces which Ayscue was transporting to Barbados. The islanders had for years relied upon Dutch ships, not English, for trade and although resentful of the heavy additional levies which Lord Willoughby had imposed upon their trading profits they feared that the London merchants might do even more. For the most part too they were loyal to the Stuarts and disgusted by the murder of Charles I.

Ayscue's small fleet appeared off Oistins or Austin's Bay on 15 October 1651 and was fortunate the next day in taking by surprise 14 ships flying the Dutch flag. Some of these were sent off by the Commonwealth admiral to bring back fresh water from neighbouring islands, while the food found aboard was distributed to feed the men in Ayscue's ships. Having secured food and drink Ayscue was able to establish an effective blockade against Barbados. It was not however until later in November that Ayscue obtained permission from his fellow Commissioners to send 200 men ashore under Captain Morris. This small detachment landed near the Hole and after a skirmish captured 30 prisoners. Nine days later and after 15 ships of a Commonwealth fleet, bound for Virginia for the reduction of more rebellious Royalists, had arrived in Carlisle Bay, a second landing of 500 men was made on the west coast near Speightstown. Its leader Colonel Alleyne met his death ashore but the soldiers, including 100 Scotsmen, captured 4 guns, 500 arms and gunpowder at Denmark Fort. An outbreak of scurvy and insufficient water for the enlarged Commonwealth troops forced the Virginia fleet to sail from Barbados on 14 December, leaving only Ayscue's ships to continue the blockade which the Royalists ashore had resisted for two months.

Unable to reduce Barbados by force, the Commonwealth commissioners in co-operation with some of the planters captured during the attack near Speightstown set up a fifth column ashore. They were helped especially by ex-governor Henry Hawley, who had a seat on the Council, and by Colonel Modyford who had grown rich from the cultivation of sugar and commanded a regiment. These influential planters persuaded other men of substance that a long blockade would have serious repercussions on trade which was already suffering from drought and the high levies. They also hinted that terms of submission to the Commonwealth might be drawn up in a way that would give protection to them as owners of property in England as well as in Barbados. And they went so far as to suggest that Barbados might obtain representation in the English Parliament.

Willoughby tried to oppose these winds of change, but on 3 January 1652 Colonel Modyford persuaded 500 infantry and 120 cavalry of the Windward men to go over to the Commonwealth side. Willoughby's efforts to smash the traitors in his camp with superior force were damped by heavy losses inflicted by Modyford's Windward men and washed out by heavy rains and mud as the heavens poured water down continuously for a week. He had to sue for peace. At the Mermaid Tavern in

Austin's Bay on 11 June 1652 articles of agreement were signed to end the war. Praised as the Charter of Barbados these articles of agreement were never honoured by the Republicans, who had no sooner got control of Barbados than they set aside the act of general indemnity and banished Willoughby and his chief supporters from Barbados.

Power in Barbados had simply been switched from one élite group to another. The republican élite, who now paid court to Governor Searle as the Commonwealth's representative, were to enjoy making profits from planting and trade as much as the Royalist élite had done under Willoughby. Their hope was that their profits would be greater because there was no Lord Willoughby to collect feudal dues. Their faith was pinned too upon article 3 of the Charter, which stipulated that 'no taxes, customs, imports, loans or excise shall be laid, nor levy made on any the inhabitants of this island without their consent in a general assembly.'

As the general assembly consisted of 22 persons chosen by themselves on the basis of two for each of 11 parishes they were confident that their will would be done there, as in Council, where 'the desire of the inhabitants' was to influence the Governor in his choice of members. The republicans in Barbados had their hands free once the struggle for power continued in England. The Rump oligarchy was no longer supreme! In the very month of August 1652 when 60 or 70 members of Parliament confirmed the Barbados Charter, the Council of English Army officers petitioned the same men to carry out a long list of delayed reforms. Cromwell as leader of the Army had come to the conclusion that England needed another strong authority to hold in check this self-perpetuating oligarchy of the Rump. In March 1653 he marched troops into the House of Commons and expelled its members. He replaced them by 130 men who were selected by his army officers for their known attachment to religion and virtue. Their rule lasted for some months until they in turn were expelled from the House of Commons in December and Cromwell became England's sole ruler with the title of Protector.

With no one to restrain him in England Cromwell, abetted by Warwick and others with overseas experience, found himself at last able to indulge his long-cherished ambition of crippling the Catholic Spanish hold on the Indies. In the autumn of 1654 he took the decision to launch his Western Design, a great raid of reprisal in the Caribbean, which could lead to a war of conquest over Spanish America, and make come true the dreams of great Elizabethan sailors like Gilbert, Drake, Raleigh, Frobisher, Cumberland and Hawkins.

Barbados, as the most highly developed of the plantations, the richest in men and resources, was chosen as the recruiting centre for the grand design. General Venables was appointed army commander, Penn admiral of the Fleet, and Governor Searle of Barbados and Edward Winslow, a former Governor of Plymouth, Massachusetts, Civil Commissioners, together with Cromwell's special representative, Gregory Butler. In addition General Venables held a special commission as overlord with full power and authority to command the several respective governors of the islands of Barbados, Bermuda and Antigua, all the Caribbee islands and all English plantations in America. Not since the Earl of Warwick's appointment in 1643 had any Englishman been entrusted with so much power over England's nascent overseas empire.

Venables arrived in Carlisle Bay on 28 January 1655 and notified the authorities there that they had to provide billets for 2500 soldiers who had been recruited in England, contribute 4000 more fighting men for his army and provide thousands of weapons, as well as pay for the entire cost of the expedition force while it remained in Barbados.

It was a brutal moment for those planters who had betrayed Willoughby and followed Colonel Modyford. They now turned against Modyford especially since he had been appointed President of the Commission which had to approach the Assembly for its support. Their rage did not lessen Venables' power however, nor were they anxious to provoke his undisciplined army which was full of Irish papist and anabaptist recruits who had no reason to love the harsh régime of the republican planters, and real incentives to stir up trouble in the island to which they had been sent as political prisoners.

Reluctantly the planters gave their quota of servants and released artisans who despite their status as freemen were heavily in debt and therefore liable for conscription. Besides quotas of men Barbados also supplied many women to go as nurses when the expedition of 60 ships left Carlisle Bay on 31 March. About 2000 arms had been commandeered for Venables' English troops and another 2500 'demi-piques' had been manufactured in Barbados. For two months instructors had drilled the men who were conscripted and even Colonel Morris' regiment of planters had turned out once a week.

When on 21 March mobilisation orders were issued for the Western Design a muster list recorded 732 officers, 5609 other ranks, 60 headquarters staff and 487 auxiliaries. Aboard the ships in Carlisle Bay there were also about 1200 sailors and crew. The expedition failed to capture Hispaniola but established a successful bridgehead upon Jamaica, when the Spanish fled into the highlands.

Barbados had received a stern example of power politics which was never to be forgotten. From the moment the military took over in 1655 a longing for independence from imperial control began to germinate. The seed took root and blossomed after the Restoration.

3 Dependence upon England

Cromwell's use of Barbados as a launching ground for his attack upon Spanish islands in the West Caribbean was a logical consequence of the Navigation Act, which the Rump Parliament had passed on 3 October 1650. The preamble of that act spelt out Parliament's attitude to the overseas plantations in words of stark clarity. They were planted 'at the cost' and 'settled' by people who 'are, or ought to be, subordinate to and dependent upon England'. They consequently ought to be 'subject to such laws, orders and regulations as are, or shall be, made by the Parliament of England'.

Having relegated the settlers to the status of subjects of Parliament the legislators of the Rump proclaimed a ban against use of foreign ships for transport of goods to and from plantations, and the nullification, at the Council of State's discretion, of all proprietary or chartered rights. Furthermore the real power of Parliament had been demonstrated by the use of English naval ships to subdue the Royalist rebels in Barbados, Antigua, Bermuda, Virginia, the Chesapeake plantations and Maryland.

Unsettled conditions inside England and involvements with Holland, France and Spain in Europe and overseas, made continuous supervision of plantations by varying governments of the Commonwealth and Protectorate impracticable. Isolated instances of showing the flag were necessarily followed by periods when representatives of the English government in the plantations were left unhindered to enrich themselves and their supporters.

The years which intervened between the departure of Venables' fleet from Bridgetown in March 1655 and the Restoration of the Stuart monarchy in 1660 were years of growth in Barbados. So great was the development of sugar plantations that the author of a description of the 'Caribby islands' in 1666 claimed that ten years since, in 1656, ships had transported from Barbados as many tons of goods yearly 'as the Spaniards did out of the former Empires of Mexico, and Perou, the Terra-firma, and out of those famous islands of Porto Rico, high Spanyola, Jamaica, when it was theirs, and Cuba'.

The rapid extension of sugar cane, accompanied by the inflow of slave workers from Africa, led to unemployment amongst white freemen. The land area of Barbados was so small that only a limited number of persons could obtain riches from exploitation of the sugar cane. Many families therefore took advantage of opportunities which were opening on sugar plantations in Surinam, Antigua and Jamaica. From this time forward Barbados began to be considered by investors in other plantations as a source of settlers of a type who were no longer available in the Mother Country. As the streams of emigrants from 'big England' dried up the men of 'little England', as Barbados began to be called, came to fill a more constructive imperial role than Oliver Cromwell and his friends had asked of them. In pursuit of greater fortunes for themselves they helped to increase the sum total of England's prosperity overseas. They were assisted by the Dutch, whose West Indian Company had since 1647 begun an 'advantageous trade in blacks' collected at assembly points of the West African coast for transportation across the Atlantic to their slave depot on Curaçao. By the time the Anglo-Dutch war ended in 1654 the Company had gained enough experience to meet the needs of all the English plantations. Their success also excited the envy of those London merchants who were waiting anxiously for a share in the large profits which could be made from the transport of human cargoes out of Africa to the Caribbees.

Slavery had been condoned for many centuries in Europe and had gained a new lease of life in the Iberian peninsula after the reconquest of its Muslim territories. It crossed the Atlantic with the Spaniards after the discovery of the Indies, black Africans replacing Moors. Slavery was vigorously condemned by two Christian priests, St Peter Claver, who spent the years 1614 to 1654 as spiritual counsellor and friend of the Africans who landed at Cartagena, and Father Antonio Vieira, who denounced the introduction of negro slavery in Brazil. Other voices of protest were added to theirs, but the voices in favour of slavery were louder still. It was not easy to persuade the conscience of man-

12   (*opposite*) *Planter's morning cup of Sangaree. From Waller's* A Voyage in the West Indies

13 *Rowlandson's caricature of Rachel Pringle Polgreen, an inn-keeper of Bridgetown, late eighteenth century*

kind that slavery was wrong in an age when soldiers were being enslaved in Scotland and when millions of agrarian serfs were virtual slaves in Eastern Europe.

English investors at home took to the slave trade as willingly as the English residents in Barbados. Both groups were tempted by its profitability and its value as a supplier of labour for plantations. The Royal Africa Company, which was formed especially to break Holland's monopoly as slave carrier to the West Indian plantations, had King Charles, his brother James and many eminent noblemen as shareholders. Later in the century too, Parliament sanctioned the slave trade as highly 'beneficial and advantageous to this kingdom and to the Plantations and colonies'.

Under such favourable auspices the popularity of slavery spread throughout the colonies, even reaching into Canada, where in 1709 an act made slavery legal. Trade in slaves not only became socially respectable during the reign of George II but opened doors for ambitious men to enter the services, marry into the nobility and even buy honours and political power. Although the reforming voices of philanthropists and vested interests had combined to end slavery into the colonies by the third decade of the nineteenth century the trade continued to flourish in America and elsewhere well in the 'eighties. Today it has not entirely been banished from the earth.

The sweet negotiation of sugar and the dark traffic in human beings brought profits to limited numbers of sugar growers and merchant traders. Their prosperity coincided with the evolution of a new political structure in England, within which capitalism could freely develop.

Meanwhile Lord Willoughby, who had been banished from the Carlisle Province by the new Commonwealth rulers of Barbados in 1652, had spent his 'exile' in England, mostly in prison. Soon after the Restoration in 1660 the death of the second Earl of Carlisle focused attention once more upon the title deeds of the Caribbees. Called in to adjudicate, the Earl of Clarendon suggested to Willoughby and the Earl of Kinnoul, who was Carlisle's immediate heir, that King Charles should take over the fiefdom originally given by his father to the first Earl of Carlisle. The King would then abdicate his new rights as lord proprietor on condition that the planters established in Barbados and other islands

D

of the Carlisle Province voted him a permanent revenue through their elective assemblies. The King would, under these conditions, agree to appoint Willoughby as governor of all the islands for several years and allow him to keep half the revenue which he collected from the Province. The remaining half would be paid, partly as pensions to the Earls of Kinnoul and Marlborough and partly to the creditors of the two Earls of Carlisle. When all the creditors had been paid off and when Willoughby's tenure of office expired the greater portion of the revenues would revert to the Crown.

These arrangements, which Willoughby accepted, put the seal on an imperial policy which had been embryonic as early as 1634. It was still potential during Warwick's administration as supreme overlord of plantations from 1643, was actually proclaimed in the Navigation Acts of 1650 and 1651, and enforced by the Commonwealth when Barbados and other rebellious Royalist plantations were reduced. Cromwell revived the policy when he made Barbados support and subsidise his attack on the Spanish Indies in 1655. Now under Charles II the imperial skeleton put on flesh and walked out of the cupboard unashamedly.

Acceptance of Clarendon's plan by Willoughby effectively made the islands royal colonies, directly dependent upon the Crown of England. Even before Clarendon's suggestion was put to Willoughby a committee of the Privy Council had been appointed to draw up policies for the plantations. They were to discover 'how best these could be made useful and beneficial to the mother country'. The implementation of these policies would be left to a Parliament which was then greatly influenced by a forward-looking group of merchants, and by officials and statesmen with imperialist vision, men like Clarendon himself, Arlington, Prince Rupert, the Duke of York and others.

Clarendon constantly encouraged the King in these years to look to his plantations for revenues and the Convention Parliament was easily persuaded to pass an Act in 1660 confirming and elaborating upon the act of 1651 with the intention of securing for the Mother Country a monopoly of raw materials from the plantations. Having secured advantages for English shipowners and the enumeration of plantation commodities for the benefit of the home traders Parliament went on in 1663 to pass an act which compelled foreign imports to pass through England as a staple.

The objects of this act left no doubt that a new era had dawned. It was intended to draw the King's subjects in the plantations closer to the Kingdom of England; 'to keep them in a firmer dependence upon it'; to make them 'more beneficial and advantageous unto it in the further employment and increase of English shipping, vent of English woolen and other manufactures and commodities'; and to follow the usage of other nations of keeping 'their plantation trade to themselves'.

It was one thing to make plans and pass legislation in England: another to implement them in the plantations. Prohibitions on trade and interference with normal patterns of demand and supply added to the losses which arose from acts of nature such as droughts, hurricanes or plant pests. Even before Lord Willoughby received the King's Commission in 1662 to go out to govern the Caribbees for seven years the price of sugar in Barbados had fallen to such a low value that in September 1661 vestries and churchwardens were authorised to levy taxes to augment the fees of ministers of religion.

By 1666 Lord Willoughby was protesting in the strongest possible terms to King Charles. 'I must and will tell the truth,' he wrote: 'Barbados, that fair jewel of His Majesty's Crown, is the best peopled spot in these parts of the world, and yields her Prince the greatest income; the gentry bred here are all lively spirited men, very industrious and the most active in improving commerce and traffic of any ever heard of'. Yet, 'free trade is the life of all colonies, but such is the condition of the Caribbee islands that they have not clothes sufficient to hide their nakedness, or food to fill their bellies. Whoever he be that advised His Majesty to restrain and tie up his colonies in point of trade is more a merchant than a good subject and would have His Majesty's islands nursed up to work for him and such men . . . there are no idle men in the island, and it ought to have a standing guard of 500 soldiers well paid with 1000 more distributed in the other Leeward islands'. He supposed they might be maintained from island revenues after the first year, if only 'His Majesty would allow them free trade, and also to Guinea for negroes, which brought them to what they are, and if not allowed again His Majesty's interest will go back as fast as it did increase.'

The man on the spot was always to find it difficult to communicate his needs convincingly to the government at home. Lord Willoughby, who had direct access to the King, suffered from the distance which separated the centre from a far point on the circumference of Empire.

The King had kept the promise which had been made to Willoughby by Clarendon. In return for an imposition of $4\frac{1}{2}\%$ to be paid in specie 'upon all dead commodities of the growth or produce' of the islands shipped abroad he abolished the existing proprietor's feudal entitlement to 40 pounds of cotton. He also permitted the islanders to hold their 'several plantations to them and to their heirs for ever in free and common socage, yielding and paying therefore at the Feast of St Michael's every year, if the same be fairly demanded, one eare of Indian corn to His Majesty, his heirs and successors for ever in full and free discharge of all rents and services.'

Thirty-six years had passed in Barbados before the settlers of cleared lands obtained permanent title deeds to them, but the burdensome export duty was to continue until the year 1838. Willoughby had been able to pass the enabling legislation through oligarchic assemblies of landowners who wanted valid title deeds to their properties. But none of the assemblies in the Caribbees had the power to reverse the duty once consent had been given. The veto of the Governor and the power of the King to make legislation null and void was stronger than the rights of Englishmen to govern themselves on plantations overseas.

The new Barbadian landowners soon found that the $4\frac{1}{2}\%$ duty was not the only imposition they would have to pay. The renewal of war with Holland and savage raids by French seamen upon some of the Leeward islands required action by Willoughby on a wide Caribbean front, so the Barbadian planters were asked to vote special grants for general defence.

It was not easy to persuade planters who for the first time felt secure in the tenures of their plantations, that even the defence of Barbados required taxes additional to $4\frac{1}{2}\%$ duty on exports. Although the Dutch Admiral De Ruyter in April 1665 damaged ships and destroyed buildings during an attack upon Bridgetown,

resentful planters still refused supplies to Willoughby and complained in a petition to the King that he was aiming to 'subvert
his Majesty's government and just rights'.

Incensed by this misinterpretation of his defence measures
Willoughby used his power to dissolve the assembly and required
the ringleaders of the opposition to his government to appear
before the next General Sessions to answer charges made against
them. One of them, Samuel Farmer, who typified the increasing
local resentment of rule from London, declared that 'he would
be damned and rot where he was' before he stopped criticising
the Governor's administration. Willoughby sent him to England
where he was kept in prison for three months before trial. He
did not return until 1667.

France's entry into the war in 1660 and the real threat to
Barbados arising from the fall of St Christopher and raids upon
Antigua and Montserrat finally persuaded the members of the
Barbadian Assembly to vote defence supplies. But not before
they had tried unsuccessfully to tie the hands of the King's representative by suggesting that the control of defence spending
should lie with a committee of three planters! The King had been
restored but the *mores* of republicanism were by now firmly
rooted in the Barbadian soil.

In his last report to the King on 15 July 1666, shortly before
sailing from Barbados to meet death by drowning off the Isles
des Saintes, Willoughby could not say too much for the islanders.
'Nor,' he wrote, 'could His Majesty do too much for them; for
having but very scant of bread to put into their mouths, yet they
have spared it out of their own bellies to set your Majesty out a
fleet and keep their people constantly at work to fortify the
island'.

His nephew, William Willoughby, who became one of four
Commissioners who held office until Lord Willoughby's death
was certified and a successor appointed, gave a more critical
appraisal of Barbados' condition in December 1666.

Of '7000 men in Barbados able to bear arms', he informed the
King, there were only '2000 whose interest and honour will
engage them to a resolute defence'. The remainder were made up
of 'small planters, formerly accounted the strength of the island,
freemen and servants, who, impoverished and discontented and

without interest or hope of benefit here, it is much to be doubted whether they will expose themselves to danger'. Accordingly he was of the opinion that the safety of Barbados and the other islands depended on His Majesty 'sending speedily ships of force to defend them'.

At the same time he did not think security of the country in the future could be guaranteed until some way was found to 'give a comfortable livelihood to the meaner sort' of people. Other measures he recommended were 'supplies of negroes on reasonable terms, restraint of depopulations, and the setting out a portion of lands, as ten acres in the hundred by the richer to the poorer; those holding it only by doing the duty of others in the militia will be the best means'. The eventual adoption of this policy was to give Barbados a supply of small farmers with roots in the soil. Their descendants survived into the troubled times of the nineteenth century and beyond.

William Willoughby's report seems to have impressed the authorities in London. They realised that the islands could not by themselves provide adequate defences against the combined attacks of Dutch and French ships of war. Orders were issued to the Duke of York to send eight more men of war to join five already operating in the Caribbean Sea and instructions were given to make war by 'small squadrons' and not by 'one entire fleet as formerly'.

The new Governor of the Caribbee islands, William, Lord Willoughby, who had been appointed to succeed his brother Francis in January 1667, was supplied with reinforcements of men and arms and given a commander, Sir Tobias Bridge to execute his orders within the island of Barbados.

The goodwill and co-operation of the Council and Assembly had been guaranteed by a gracious letter from the King which had encouraged the Governor, Council and Assembly to declare that 'all laws passed in the reign of Charles I and of his present Majesty that stand unrepealed shall be taken to be the laws in force, and that the inhabitants shall be governed as heretofore, according to the laws of England and the constitutions and laws of this island'.

The new mood of the Assembly is reflected in a Council minute dated early in 1667. It records a 'cheerful' vote by the Assembly of 'sugar for setting forth a fleet for the preservation of the Leeward Isles'.

Cheerfulness is missing from Lord Willoughby's private communication to the King in midsummer. He found the island in such disorder that 'had he been an enemy, with the small force' which he brought from England 'he could have made a fair push for it'. Also he could discover no more than 4000 effective fighting men ashore!

Worse was to follow. Willoughby was of the opinion that the plantations were suffering from two needs which he prayed the King to remedy speedily. They wanted free trade with Scotland, which formerly supplied 'brave servants and faithful subjects'. And they wanted free trade to Guinea for negroes 'by which they may be as plentifully furnished as formerly'. He noted that they were now so scarce and dear that 'the poor planters will be forced to go to foreign plantations for a livelihood'. Willoughby's letter to the King was followed by a petition in September from the representatives in the Assembly. They wanted 'freedom to trade with Scotland and Guinea and in addition wanted to export commodities to any place in amity with England'. They also requested that no person should be expelled from the island to answer charges in any other place, and that they might set up a mint to coin money 'to be only current in Barbados'.

Hopes of better times had soared high when Charles II conferred seven baronetcies and six knighthoods on Royalist planters in 1661. Seven years later disillusioned representatives of the people, resentful of the heavy impositions and restrictions which an ever-tightening imperial policy required of them, asked the King for a charter which two centuries later would have been described as 'dominion status'. Not surprisingly King Charles reminded the islanders in 1671 of their obligations as subjects, telling them through their deputy governor, that 'distance of place shall shelter none from our justice and power'.

The wheels of change revolved very speedily in the early years of Barbados' new status as a Crown Colony. The dominant vibrations came from forces outside the control of any of the Caribbee islanders, whose mainsprings of action became increasingly insular and isolationist as the imperial mood of expansion and competition against French and Dutch mercantilism stiffened.

While Barbadians were resentful of the irksome controls imposed by England's rulers, English merchants and planters trading to the Leewards had petitioned the King in 1667 to be free of the Barbadian yoke, to be in short 'no longer under the government of Barbados'. The Barbadian planters and traders for their part were also weary of the responsibilities which had been thrust upon them for protection of the Leewards and other Caribbean places under the government of the Lords Willoughby, and earlier Lieutenants General of the Caribbees.

They resented especially the constant drain of men taken for expeditions or settlements. Between 1643 and 1647, 1200 Barbadians had gone off to New England and 600 to Trinidad and Tobago. From 1646 to 1658 Virginia and Surinam had attracted 2400. Between 1650 and 1662 expeditions to Guadeloupe, Martinique, Grenada, Tobago and Curaçao had required 1600; Venables had recruited 3300 for the Western Design of 1655; Francis, Lord Willoughby had taken 1300 to St Lucia; Major Scott had recruited 800 to fight the Dutch in Tobago and Guiana in 1665, and Lord Willoughby and his nephew had taken 3000 more to fight the French in the same year. Constant expenditures were also required to arm men and equip fleets.

Finally Barbadians had to bear the cost of maintaining Sir Tobias Bridge's regiment. The loss of the Leeward islands, which became a separate government in 1671, did at least offer hope of a reduction of financial levies.

The break with the Leeward islands ended a long chapter of rivalry between plantations which grew competitive crops for a common feudal lord but which were too far apart to develop common interests. Effectively those who ruled in each island managed their own affairs from the earliest days of settlement and thought of themselves as Englishmen whose presence on plantations did not in any way debar them from the rights which would have been theirs had they remained at home.

In seeking to be free from the government of Barbados the Leewards men were asking for no more than the Barbadians had asked in 1650 when as 'free-born Englishmen' they demanded that 'liberty which is given to Englishmen at home' and requested 'the High Court of Parliament to incorporate Barbados into the Commonwealth as any town city shire or island' was incorporated at home.

It was the *liberty of Englishmen*, not political independence, which was cherished by Englishmen on plantations. It was liberty, not constitutional progress, which their descendants and other subjects of English monarchs were to seek over the long centuries in which they were satellites of the world's greatest Empire.

To preserve that liberty in the late seventeenth century and for most of the eighteenth it seemed logical to most men in power that imperial protection required plantations to produce revenues for the Home Government, if the Home Government was to supply ships to protect the trade of the plantations. Until these two essentials had been provided all talk of 'liberties' was idle chatter. The world was not ripe for democracy nor self-govern-ment. It was an age of absolute monarchs, and Barbados was only a small cog in a new imperial machine. Just another plantation overseas!

4 Decline of the Oligarchs

The role of Barbados as a pace setter in tropical plantations began to recede in the last decades of the seventeenth century, but the colony was to remain for more than a century an important linch-pin in the chain of imperial trade and defence. Because it was for some years the most prosperous of the slave-purchasing plantations, Barbados also contributed towards the expansion of British exports to Africa. African entrepreneurs were in the habit of paying for British goods by the sale of their captives to slave traders. At the same time Barbados was dependent upon the northern English mainland plantations for supplies of bread, drink, fish, meat, horses, timber and staves.

The English mercantile system was a unified trading system mutually beneficial to all units af an expanding Empire. It was not until late in the eighteenth century that the hegemony of Barbados and other British West Indian plantations in this trading pattern began to diminish because of a slow rate in growth of white population as compared with a rapid increase on the northern mainland colonies. By 1750 more than one million white inhabitants were living in the North American colonies as compared with no more than 40,000 who were scattered around the British West Indian islands.

The static or contracting size of the European population in Barbados was due chiefly to high mortality rates, emigration and recruitment for military expeditions. So serious was the exodus of whites that an act was passed in August 1670 to 'Prevent Spiriting People' off the island. Anyone found guilty of such an offence was to be sentenced 'to stand in the Pillory in some public place in the Town of St Michael's for three several days with a paper on his head in great letters, declaring the said deceit and to receive 20 lashes on the bare back'.

In view of the anxiety about loss of population the departure of Sir John Colleton in 1669 with a party of settlers for Charles Town in Carolina was ill-timed.

Planters were by this time also very fearful of negro uprisings. A visitor from England in 1662 had noted that many thousands of slaves could speak English. He accurately described the fears of the planters and merchants when he emphasised the constant danger of slaves rising in support of invading troops and forcibly warned that, 'should Holland or France or both gain Barbados, its situation, wealth and trade would make them masters of the West Indies'.

The danger of slave risings was not likely to be lessened by the new guidelines which the Home Government had given to William Lord Willoughby. In 1667 he had been directed in his commission to encourage instruction of slaves in the doctrines of the Church of England. At the same time Charles II had made clear that admission to the sacraments was not to be followed by enfranchisement or manumission in the islands. Planters quickly recognised in the tenets of Christianity a challenge to their future security as masters and discouraged the implementation of the royal instructions. It was however easier for Lord Willoughby to 'encourage' the teaching of Christian doctrine to slaves than to carry out another instruction which commanded him to prevent the departure of freemen from the island. Nor was it easy to ensure that small plantations which usually maintained one family were not 'added to great ones'. Before the institution of modern police forces it was a simple matter to steal away from any West Indian island by boat.

The overriding fear of the planters for several decades of the late seventeenth century and early eighteenth century was the possibility of attacks by sea. Privateers roamed the Caribbean in peace time and French fleets had to be warded off in time of war. The British navy was incapable of guarding all the British islands from assault until Rodney's momentous victory over de Grasse near the Isles des Saintes during the war of the American Revolution. British sea power was never invincibly established in the Caribbean before Nelson's victory off Trafalgar in 1805. Yet as Christopher Codrington wrote in 1690: 'All turns on mastery of the sea. If we have it our islands are safe, however thinly peopled; if the French have it, we cannot, after the recent mortality, raise enough men in all the islands to hold one of them.'

The French shared Codrington's views. Father Labat, the martial Dominican priest who visited Barbados at the end of the century, stole a plan of the island and made detailed notes of its fortifications and militia. He considered that the French could capture Barbados with about 5000 Creoles and filibusters provided that a dozen French warships were sent in support.

Between 1688 and 1815 England was at war for a total of 64 years, and in seven great wars with France; the shortest lasted seven and the longest 12 years. It was during this century and a half of constant preoccupation with defence that Barbados was gradually made into what George Washington described in 1751 as an 'intire fortification'. Already by 1670 the work was far advanced. Colonel Robert Rich in a letter dated 31 May of that year recorded that Bridgetown, which was then called St Michael's, had '2 forts and a platform between, all well fortified and stocked with great guns.' Another two forts and platform, equally well furnished with great guns were established at Oistins, which then contained many storehouses and was a relatively important harbour for trading ships. St James' Town, as Holetown was then called, had one 'very large platform and breast works' and Speightstown, the second largest port and trading centre, had 'two well-built strongly fortified forts'. Rich's estimate of the militia then available for defending Barbados against invaders was '2 regiments of horse and 5 regiments of foot'. He estimated the total population to be 60,000, of whom one third were blacks and mulattos and some were 'Jews, Dutch or French'. The majority were English, Scotch and Irish. The island at the time produced muscovado, clayed and refined sugar as good as 'any in the world', but was still exporting ginger, indigo and 'cotton wool'. Rum was drunk 'in great abundance' by servants and slaves but exports of this 'spirit of the sugar cane' were also made to Virginia, Bermuda and New England.

From New England, Ireland, Virginia, Bermuda and Newfoundland the islanders obtained beef, pork, fish, peas, flour, butter, cheese and 'bisquet', as well as timber, boards, staves, pipes and hogsheads. New England and the Cape Verde islands also sent bulls, cows, assinegos and horses. Guinea supplied negro slaves, and 'old England' sent 'servants' and all other commodities for plantations and for apparel. About 200 vessels, ketches, sloops and barges mostly of English registry called yearly and every ship had to pay one pound of powder per ton to keep the 'magazine' well stored.

The majority of ships took on sugar for England, but some went for New England, Bermuda, Virginia, Tangier and other foreign ports. If ships were plentiful rates were sometimes £3 or less per ton, more usually £4 to £5. When ships were scarce rates rose to £6 or £7, and in the 'late war with the Dutch' went to £10, £11 or £12 per ton!

War put up the cost of living, plague and other diseases cut short life, while fires, explosions, hurricanes and earthquakes occurred with terrifying frequency. In 1668 Major James Beane noted that not a twentieth part of the houses in St Michael's Town had escaped the blaze which began in the house of Messrs Bond and Bushell and spread to a magazine stored with over 200 barrels of gunpowder. The magazine blew up, nearly 100 houses were burnt down and the loss was estimated at over £300,000. As if mutilation of its town by fire was not enough the year 1668 was one of blistering drought. The rains failed, Lord Willoughby ruefully reported to London, because the island had been 'encloathed of its woods'. The 'thickets' were so burnt up, he said, that people were ready to 'desert the plantations.' The rains came with fury seven years later, on 31 August 1675, even dragging coffins from the churchyards on to the beaches. Sugar works and dwelling houses were blown down, ships were washed ashore, canes were bent flat in the fields, corn fields were waterlogged and crops ruined, curing houses were damaged, churches and windmills were levelled to the ground. So great was the damage that the 'best planters had to live in huts' and 'were afraid to build high houses for a long time after'.

The Quakers, who had heard George Fox preach in Barbados in 1671, may well have regarded the awful hurricane of 1675 as a punishment for the way negroes and Indians were neglected by the 'ministers, teachers and priests' in Barbados. 'Is not the Gospel to be preached to all Creatures?' Fox had asked them. 'And are they not men? And are they not part of your families?' These were awkward questions to put to the men who had failed to carry out Charles II's instructions as detailed in the commission granted to William Lord Willoughby.

In revenge the authorities wreaked vengeance upon some Quakers, bringing them before a Grand Jury in 1673 and accusing others of stirring 'the blacks' to rebellion. Despite legislation which was passed in 1676 to prevent attendance of slaves at meeting houses of Friends, the Quakers persisted in their humanitarian efforts which were at least a century ahead of the average 'enlightened' opinions of most liberal-minded Europeans.

The planters were too frightened to be philosophical and when a slave rising was discovered in May of 1675 the government ordered the execution of 35 ringleaders who had been betrayed by a woman slave who feared for her kind master's life. Ferocity in repression was doubtless due to fears as to the likely behaviour of transported Irish and convicted white felons who had little cause to love their masters on the plantations and who were expected to assist rebellious slaves as well as foreign invaders. Repressive acts were also common in eighteenth-century Europe. The English in Barbados were men of their age. For many more centuries labourers were to be considered 'outside the nation' in Europe and were treated as serfs unless they owned land. Punishments too were brutal. A warrant for a multiple execution at Bath in 1685 required 'faggots to burn the bowels of 4 traitors, a furnace or cauldron to boil their heads and quarters, and salt to boil these with, half a bushel to each traitor, and tar to tar them with'. Labourers were executed in England as late as 1830, after a rebellion, while seamen were frequently flogged to death. It was not until 1821 that the number of strokes which might be given to seamen were limited to 300! In 1833 a boy of 9 was sentenced to death in England for stealing printer's ink valued at twopence, and 'drawing, beheading and quartering' were on the statute books till 1870. So deep-rooted were European prejudices against persons who did not belong to the establishment, that it seems remarkable that the oligarchs of Barbados should have approved legislation in 1805 making the murder of a slave a capital offence!

Probably because of the relatively large number of ships which called at Barbados the island was often liable to epidemics brought in from overseas. At least 6000 'Christians' had died in 1648, large numbers had fled to Nevis in the winter of 1670, and in 1691 about one third of all the inhabitants perished through fever. For decades there was a heavy toll from the mysterious and dreaded 'belly ache' disease which later medical science supposes to have been caused by lead poisoning due to drinking rum which had been distilled in leaden pipes.

By 1684 Barbados had 844 plantations and by 1690 all of the machinery used in the manufacture of sugar was of English design. The census of 1683 enumerated 17,187 free inhabitants and 2,381 white bond servants. Only 4,056 persons were householders so the majority of the whites at the time must have worked for wages around the towns or as labourers or tenant farmers on plantations.

While the wheel of Barbadian fortunes continued to spin unevenly, interspersed by calamitous occurrences, the rise of England's economy was on the way. Between 1660 and 1700 the value of England's imports and exports rose by 50%, its customs revenues trebled and its merchant marine more than doubled in size. Advance was also being recorded by England's greatest European rival. By the 1680's the France of Louis XIV owned trading posts in India, island stations in the Indian Ocean, slaving stations in Africa and a number of plantations on important Caribbean islands.

Both the rival European powers now set high store on their Caribbean islands, regarding them as valuable trading units and important strategic outposts of expanding imperial systems. Power was openly recognised to be the real aim of national policies, and the Caribbean was the traditional area where the rival maritime powers fought their sea battles. Because of the contests for control of the sea waged between France and England over the years 1689 to 1815 English planters in the Caribbean had to seek English naval protection as their first requirement for survival.

The mercantile system, which England had taken over from Colbert and improved upon, reached fruition in the Navigation Act of 1696, which gave revenue officers in colonies powers of entry and search of business houses equivalent to those held by customs officers in England. Under the terms of this act plantation goods could not be landed in Scotland or Ireland, foreigners were forbidden to acquire property in colonies, and colonial legislation repugnant to English laws of trade were made void. Unable to achieve through their Assembly the rights which English gentlemen were winning through their House of Commons Barbadian planters thought it prudent to claim rights as English gentlemen who had investments in colonial plantations. To make sure that their voices could be heard in Parliament they appointed Edward Littleton and William Bridges to be their agents in London in 1691. A similar policy had been adopted earlier by several American colonies.

The last decade of the seventeenth century was a time of great troubles. In 1692 Barbadian planters and merchants had to fit out two large ships to guard their shores from prowling enemy vessels, the sugar crop failed, there was a raging pestilence and the slaves plotted a general insurrection. Property owners also had to supply 'comfortable lodgings' and food for English troops quartered upon them, while they lost 1400 men as recruits to Sir Francis Wheeler's expedition against Martinique.

There was near panic on the island when in 1696 a French fleet was sighted, but the French did not attack. They had no means of knowing that Barbadian forts then only contained seven rounds of powder! Bridgetown was an impressive enough city from the sea, as Samuel Copen's map of 1695 shows. It was a typical Dutch-style, seventeenth-century seaport with red tiled roofs, brick chimneys, wharves and quays. Its bay was full of ships riding at anchor, its forts looked substantial and its inner harbour was larger than today's because it had a molehead projecting far out to sea and was protected by a barrier reef at the north of the town. Its appearance justifies the praise which was lavished upon it by Father Labat. He wrote in 1700: 'The houses are well built in the English style with many glass windows; they are magnificently furnished. The shops and merchants' warehouses are filled with all one could wish from all parts of the world . . . the largest trade in America is carried on here . . . one notices the opulence and good taste of the inhabitants in their magnificent furniture and silver of which they all have considerable quantities'.

It was in this fair city that the authorities put on an elaborate ceremony for the Duke of Portland in November 1721 when he called with his duchess, and his daughter Lady Ann Bentinck on their way to Jamaica. As they stepped ashore the ladies and their

14   *and 15 (opposite) Above: Ogilvy's map of Barbados as it was in the late seventeenth century. Below: Spanish map of same period*

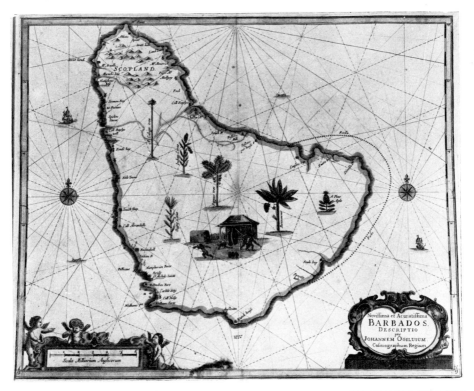

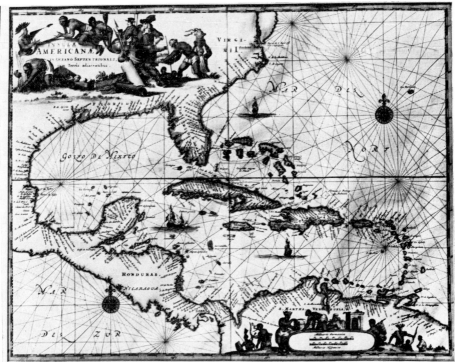

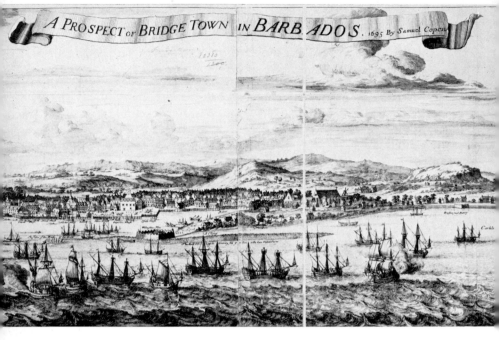

16   Samuel Copen's prospect of Bridgetown, 1695

17   British troops parade on Garrison Savannah, late nineteenth century

attendants were handed into coaches drawn by six horses; behind them the Duke walked on the right of President Cox through the principal streets of Bridgetown to the President's House, followed by his attendants, the Members of the Council and Assembly and the Life Guards of Horse. Several companies of militia lined the streets to watch the ducal procession. The balconies were filled with people of the best fashion who came from all parts of the island to be spectators of a sight the like of which had not been seen since the Duke and Duchess of Albemarle visited Bridgetown in 1687. Twenty years later Bridgetown is described as having 1200 houses built of stone, with glazed and sashed windows. Its streets are said to be 'broad, the houses high, and the rents as dear in Cheapside in the Bridge as in Cheapside in London'. The tradesmen's shops were as well furnished as the shops and warehouses of London, there were several large taverns and eating houses, and a post house for the receipt of letters from all parts.

Nearly 40 years later on 10 October 1780 this town of broad streets and attractive store houses was reduced to a mass of ruins and rubble by a hurricane. Not more than 30 houses and stores were left standing. The steeple of St Michael's cathedral toppled, the expensive molehead was destroyed, the inner basin of the harbour was filled with sand, stones and timber, castles, forts, batteries, town hall, prison and the general's residence were blown down. The streets reeked of dead bodies and rotting fish. At least 3,000 persons were killed and all but three churches were made unfit for worship. It was the most devastating single catastrophe ever experienced in Barbados, and Bridgetown never recovered from the disaster. Estimates of the loss exceed many millions of pounds in today's currency, but the major loss was the character of a town which combined the efficiency of a Dutch port with the elegance of English eighteenth century standards of living. For in this period of time some English standards of elegance had penetrated into Barbados. This was the time when an English visitor wrote that 'masters, merchants and planters lived each like little sovereigns in their plantations . . . their tables are spread every day with variety of nice dishes . . . their equipages are rich, their liveries fine . . . their chairs, chaises and all the conveniences for their travelling magnificent. The most wealthy of them besides this land train have their pleasure boats

E

to make the tour of their island in and sloops to convey their goods to and from the Bridge. Their dress and that of their ladies is fashionable and courtly; and being generally bred at London, their behaviour is genteel and polite, in which they have the advantage of most of our country gentlemen, who living at great distances from London frequent the world very little, and from conversing always with their dogs, horses and rude peasants acquire an air suitable to them . . . the gentlemen of Barbados are civil, generous, hospitable and very sociable.'

Although many Barbadians today still pride themselves on their hospitality and social graces few of their ancestors owned lands in the eighteenth century. Some families can trace their ancestry back to the first century of settlement, but the great majority of those who have achieved prosperity in this century are descendants of persons who were brought or came to Barbados as labourers or artisans. Throughout the centuries there has been a conspicuous emigration from Barbados to other places which offered greater outlets for talent than could be provided by so limited a land area. As the English Empire expanded during the eighteenth century this outward movement increased. There was as well a slower influx of newcomers from neighbouring islands, the Americas, Ireland, Scotland and England.

By the mid-eighteenth century a specific Barbadian way of life was evolving. Trade retained priority over everything and material prosperity was the goal of all freemen. For the majority of white poor, servants and slaves, moments of happiness might be snatched when there was a lull in pestilences, no food shortages, no alarums from enemy ships, no hurricanes and no rebellions. Life for the underdogs of society was at least as tolerable in Barbados as it was in most agricultural communities, while the blessings of sea and sun were bonuses.

Some topics which concerned the men who represented the small body of electors may be glimpsed from a look at some of the Acts they passed in Assembly. In 1719 there was apprehension that a spiritual court would be established so special legislation was needed to calm 'terrors and apprehensions'. Six years later Quakers were offered greater tolerance than before when legislators consented to let them make solemn affirmation and declaration in lieu of oaths in courts. A year later there was great concern about the wicked destruction of fish which was being poisoned by manchineel juice. Then followed a whole series of acts which were designed to make the maximum use of the island's resources and to control abuses. The export of clay, for instance, was forbidden by an Act of 1736 in order to safeguard the refining of sugar in clay pots. Meat prices were controlled a year later (beef at 6d per lb. and pork at 4d!) The following year legislation frowned upon the export of cattle and encouraged the raising of local herds. In 1748 an act was proclaimed to encourage the destruction of rats with an offer of 2d per head to any black or white catcher. A spate of acts were passed which today would be described as industrial incentives. In 1751 Major James Barry was encouraged by a special act to continue improvement of windmill vanes or points. A year later encouraging legislation was passed to help John Pas in the projection of an engine for the drawing of water out of ponds and other places. In that year of 1752 an act was passed to reduce the rate of interest to 6%. It remained on the statute book until a few years preceding independence in 1966.

Other persons encouraged by legislation during the 1750s, which were years of Barbadian inventions, were John Stalker for projecting a hydraulic machine to raise water from any depths, Dr William Culpeper for making most useful stills and still heads for distillation of rum and other spirituous liquors, James Barry for a machine which treated trash in sugar mills, Edward Pare for building a kiln to burn lime, John Mayers, Alexander M'Cragh and Edward Lascelles Mayers of St Philip for making and refining sea salt, and Samuel Sainthill for inventing a windmill for beating out corn. The eighteenth century, which was to witness the transformation of England from a land of hundreds of small villages into a country of great industrial cities, was for Barbados an age of invention as the 'little Englanders' struggled to adapt to new winds of change blowing across the Atlantic from Europe.

The years of peace with France 1749-55 were probably the best that Barbados had experienced since the golden decade of sugar ended a hundred years before. During the Seven Years War Barbados had to look hard at its defences and in 1761 contributed £24,000 to send a regiment against Martinique. The strength of its own armed forces was still effective in 1775. But a year earlier

America declared independence and set in motion a train of events which caused the dissolution of a compact and profitable trade between the North American and Caribbean colonies. In 1775 Barbados could still impress the King's geographer Thomas Jeffreys, who noted six regiments of infantry, three of cavalry and one troop of guards, 'all stout men and well disciplined'. Jefferys expressed approval of that early agrarian law which gave every servant three or four acres of land at the expiration of indenture and provided the yeomanry or militia, which he called 'one of the most respected in the West Indies'.

A year later the British embargo on America's trade deprived Barbados of essential food. White poor as well as negroes were hungry for a time, while food prices soared 150% and corn, when available, cost 400% more than usual. In panic Barbadians took sail for St Lucia. It was said that there were insufficient men left to protect the island from invasion. Hard times persisted until the island's economy was shattered by the murderous hurricane of 1780. There was some alleviation when Rodney captured St Eustatius in 1781 and sent back goods and materials to Bridgetown. In the spring of 1782, when Rodney saved Jamaica by defeating de Grasse off the islets of the Saintes, hopes stirred in Barbadian breasts that the wheel of prosperity would turn once again in their favour. Yet the doom of their economy had been written when the secession of the first mainland American colonies confirmed Adam Smith's earlier assumption that 'Great Britain derives nothing but loss from the dominion which she assumes over her colonies'.

Though some Englishmen in office believed that the restrictions on the American Republic's trade with the British islands would encourage Canada to take its place as supplier to the West Indies and purchaser of their exports, such a development was impossible for economic reasons. The anaemic West Indian economy managed to keep a pulse of trade flickering for a while because a blind official eye was often turned by English customs administrators in the islands to embargoes decreed from London. Privateers who traded illegally throughout the Caribbean in collusion with American shipowners kept the planters and merchants from total collapse. Other ideas were also at work undermining traditional views of colonies, especially with respect to the use of human forced labour as an essential ingredient of economic prosperity upon plantations. Any hopes which the planters might have entertained from the British navy's victory over the French, any dreams of a new golden age for sugar faded as the conscience of western man rebelled against the enslavement of blacks for the enrichment of whites.

The end of the slave trade, which was proclaimed by Great Britain in 1806, was followed in 1832 by the beginning of reform of the British parliament and in 1833 by the abolition of slavery throughout the British Empire. Ever since 1772 Lord Mansfield's judgement that a human being could not be regarded as a slave on English soil foreshadowed the extension of a similar principle to the overseas dependencies of Britain. When the end came in 1833 the old plantation system under which men from England invested overseas to create wealth and revenue for England was no more. Unfortunately for those who remained in the West Indies most of the compensation for the capital loss of slaves was paid to creditors of the plantations resident in England and the islanders were left to pull themselves up by their own bootstraps. Their condition was not helped by the massive destruction of property suffered during the terrible hurricane of 1831. Yet for the first time in centuries of oppression the servile population of Barbados had something better to contemplate than perpetual slavery. Whatever the future might bring for the ex-slaves they were no longer to be goods and chattels of white men. The days of the oligarchs were numbered.

5 End of a Beginning

The negro, as distinct from the 'coloured' West Indian, knew no glorious past in fact or fiction. Negroes were defined by law as goods and chattels for hundreds of years and not until the 'forties of the present century was their entitlement to equal shares of citizenship recognised by electoral reforms in the West Indies. The political history of the West Indies is largely for these reasons the history of minorities ruling majorities.

In 1854, 20 years after negroes were made free by legislation, only 1,359 persons were registered as voters in Barbados. Of this small number only 78 went to the polling booths that year. Representation in the legislature remained the prerogative of property owners. The Queen's representative in Barbados and the Windward Islands was under no delusion as to his particular duties as Governor and Commander-in-Chief. Sir William Colebrooke reported in 1854 that the principles of responsible or party government were inapplicable to 'these small communities'. Colebrooke wanted to establish a general legislature for Barbados and the Windward Islands which would be nominated by Governors and Assemblies from all the component islands, and he suggested the creation of an Executive Council which would be selected by the Governor-in-Chief with the sole right of initiating money votes. The Canadian-born Francis Hincks, who succeeded Colebrooke as Governor, did not share his forward-looking views and the republican-minded Assemblies were allowed to persevere in their isolationist attitudes. In Barbados the idea of closer union became so repugnant that the Windward Islands ceased to be associated with its government in 1885.

Insofar as there was a planned imperial policy for the West Indies after slavery and apprenticeship were abolished, it was hopefully aimed at subduing the power of local Assemblies. The appointment in 1833 of Sir Lionel Smith was a straw in the wind.

For the first time a governor's salary came from funds at the disposal of the British Parliament, and his powers over Barbados, St Vincent, Grenada and Tobago were designed to emphasise new concepts of administrative efficiency. The combination of offices in one individual who was not dependent upon island Assemblies' approval for his pay, was a warning that local interests would no longer be permitted to override imperial edicts.

By 1844 the new policy had progressed to the point where Sir Charles Grey was recommending to the Home authorities the formation of a province of five Windward Islands sharing common institutions and laws. Barbados was to be the capital. Sir Charles urged upon the Barbadian House of Assembly the advantages of sharing 600,000 acres of fertile lands of which not more than one-third was then being cultivated. But he received no support from the isolationist House, although he had prefaced his proposal with exceeding flattery. 'You have', he told representatives of the Barbadian landed gentry, 'already the right to say that you and your predecessors on this island have made a portion of that African people to whom the West Indies are so deeply indebted for whatever riches they possess, the happiest individuals of their whole innumerable race, which now spreads from the Red Sea to the Andes; that they are in all respects the most favourable specimen of that race which exists, and the most full of promise for the future'.

The wary Barbadians, conscious of the new trends in Britain's imperial trading policy which forced their sugar to compete with sugar grown by slave labour on foreign plantations, acknowledged the governor's tribute to their exemplary treatment of their African people but asked no larger future for Barbados 'than that she may continue to move in her present orbit, with her light undimmed and her usefulness and importance undiminished'.

Their attitude was traditional, but they may have been influenced by developments in England. Charles Buller's *Mr Mother Country Of The Colonial Office* had been published in 1840 and would have been read by Barbadian legislators. Buller described Mr Mother Country as 'exercising supremacy and maintaining connections with vast widely scattered colonies in some back room in London.' Robert Lowe went further in 1844. He described governors as being responsible to clerks of the Colonial Office who were responsible to a Colonial Secretary, who was in turn responsible to an Assembly chosen for every conceivable reason except their knowledge of colonial affairs. It was not until 1854 that the Colonial Office was detached from the War Office and achieved a separate identity of its own, although a special department for Colonial affairs had been created during the momentous years 1768 to 1782.

In 1759 the elder Pitt defended the sugar colonies in Parliament in words which no longer reflected the views of the cliques who then ruled England. Their produce, Pitt said, 'was the labour of our own people . . . they are supplied with everything from hence . . . they send home all their produce and are the support of our marine . . . the landed gentlemen seemed to consider themselves in a separate interest from the colonies,' but he 'should ever consider the colonies as the landed interest of this Kingdom and it was a barbarism to consider them otherwise'.

Ninety years later, in 1849, the planters in sugar colonies were experiencing serious economic difficulties largely caused by the policies of an imperial Parliament in which they had no representation. Their spokesmen had to stand in long queues waiting for the attention of a Colonial Office whose duties were beyond the abilities of any ordinary man.

Sir William Molesworth at the time described a Colonial Secretary as a man 'traversing and retraversing in his imagination the terraqueous globe, flying from the Arctic to the Antarctic, hurrying from the snows of North America to the burning regions of the tropics; rushing across from the fertile islands of the West Indies to the arid deserts of South Africa and Australia; like nothing on earth or in romance save the Wandering Jew.' Such an individual was unlikely ever to be in a position to represent adequately the interests of Britons overseas against the ever-increasing decisions made by the Home Parliament, the Home Cabinet or the Home Sovereign.

Yet the English in Barbados cared chiefly that their light should shine undimmed and their usefulness and importance remain undiminished, so deeply ingrained were their convictions that Englishmen born in Barbados had special claims upon the Mother Country. Had not Dr Pinckard been asked in 1805: 'What would poor old England do were Barbados to forsake her?' Bereft of influence in imperial policies, forced to obey imperial edicts, the Barbadian oligarchs of the nineteenth century clung to their English birthrights as their last defence in a world which no longer cared about them.

Great Britain had repealed the $4\frac{1}{2}$% duties on exports from the Caribbee islands in 1838 and this concession was later followed by repeal of the Navigation Acts in 1849. Unfortunately by 1852 the Sugar Duties Act was also repealed and West Indian sugar growers had to sell their produce on equal terms with slave-grown sugar. Such was the penalty of free trade for outposts of Empire, within which trade no longer followed the flag. The independence of the United States had been followed by the independence of the Latin American countries. British trade flourished with both groups of these former colonies. Free trade was seen to provide greater outlets for manufacturers than were obtained under protection. Even Disraeli, who was later to make his Queen Empress of India, lamented in 1852 that 'these wretched colonies will all be independent in a few years, and they are a millstone around our necks'.

The dominant imperial concept of the unimportance of colonies in general during the mid-nineteenth century boded ill for the tiny island of Barbados, which prided itself on being as truly English as the Mother Country. Because they clung so stubbornly to outdated concepts of the rights of Englishmen living overseas and because they regarded the 1652 articles of surrender as the permanent charter or liberties of property owners, the oligarchs who ruled Barbados in the nineteenth century transmitted a fatal political legacy to the whites who succeeded them as controllers of the political Assembly in the early decades of the twentieth century. Instead of leading a wider confederation of Windward Islands into a modern world the Barbadian oligarchs resisted every attempt of the Colonial Office or its representatives to involve them in a West Indian policy which alone could bring them to the status of a self-governing dominion within the framework of Empire; and because of their isolation by sea from other Caribbean islands the Barbadian landowners of the twentieth century looked only to England as their motherland, while the children of impoverished whites streamed in ever-increasing numbers outwards to Canada, the United States, South Africa,

Australia or to wherever in a far-flung Empire they would find acceptance as white subjects of the British monarch. Caught between constant fears of falling below the depressed living standards of the children of former slaves and their needs to be preferred as employees of more prosperous whites, the majority of impoverished whites in Barbados encouraged their children to emigrate. Those who remained found it prudent to avoid confrontation with white superiors on whose goodwill alone they depended for employment. The small number of impoverished whites who achieved the status of property owners through skills and hard work were often able to infiltrate into the ruling oligarchy through business mergers or marriages. Deprived of similar openings the prosperous coloured Barbadians tended to become militant politicians. They were otherwise doomed to live as lower grade citizens in a community where they felt entitled to all the privileges of white property owners. Several had taken advantage of improved local educational facilities and others attended schools, universities and inns of court in the Mother Country; to be regarded as social inferiors on their return by a large number of whites who had not enjoyed their social advantages was particularly galling for them.

Barriers arising from differences of skin colour prevented the integration of a property-owning democracy recruited from all shades of the social rainbow. A closed society dominated by white property owners wanted above everything to preserve its privileges in local government, in the professions, in the civil service, in business, in the Assembly and in the Legislative Council. Possession of 'great' houses and country estates was regarded as evidence of a gentility which was most passionately pursued where it was least evident. To be a Barbadian gentleman, these oligarchs believed, was to be the equal of any squire or country gentleman in England and to be knighted for public services in Barbados was to be acknowledged as a member of the inner circle of rulers of Empire.

Sadly in the early decades of the twentieth century the nature of Barbadian society still encouraged the hardening of political tradition into rigid defence of past privileges, whereas everyone would have gained from enlargement of social privileges for all men and women fitted by talent and education to build a healthy multi-coloured integrated society. Those who condemn the Barbadian whites for their failure to achieve such an ideal society ought however to remember that the race tensions in Barbados never reached proportions comparable to those which elsewhere have befouled human relationships in the twentieth century.

Until 30 November 1966 those who exercised power in Barbados were always subject to certain restraints and influences emanating from the Home Country. Several of these influences notably improved the quality of life in Barbados especially during the nineteenth century. A decisive turn for the better was first made in 1825 when an Anglican bishop arrived. From that year may be noticed a pronounced official tendency to think of people as members of a community and not as essential cogs of an economic machine which was geared to the production of wealth for small minorities. The age of reform which now began in the homeland had echoes in far away Barbados, where some leaders of opinion began to share Gladstone's vision of an imperial idea born of 'what inwardly binds men and communities together'.

In 1834 slavery ended and in 1838 the apprenticeship system was abolished. A police force was established in 1835, a Chief Justice was appointed in 1841 and in 1843 the first coloured gentleman, Samuel Jackson Prescod, was elected to fill one of the two newly created seats for the City of Bridgetown. In 1848 the currency of Barbados was assimilated to that of the Mother Country. In 1852 a Savings Bank was established, internal post offices were opened and the first lighthouse erected. In 1858 the first agricultural Exhibition was held at Government House. The first issue of Barbados postage stamps was made in 1858 and in 1861 Bridgetown was supplied with water from pipes. In 1865 the centre of Bridgetown was embellished with a fountain and in 1866 the lower end of Broad Street was provided with the Montefiore Fountain, which has since been moved to face the law-courts and public library. Harrison College, the chief secondary school for boys in Barbados moved to its present site in 1871 and a year later the House of Assembly vacated the Tavern where it had met since 1792, for the Assembly Hall in Bridgetown's Public Buildings. The same year saw the opening of a telegraph service to the island. In 1875 Bridgetown was first lit by gas and in 1877 the first sod of the railway was turned. The line which ran for several decades between Bridgetown and Belle-plaine was opened in 1882. Elementary education was introduced in 1878 and a boys' reformatory in 1883.

All these reforms took place against the background of a sluggish economy in an island periodically assaulted by fires, pestilence, hurricane, earthquake, drought and other calamities. In 1838 out of 100,000 acres under cultivation 40,000 were under sugar cane. Barbados had received compensation of £1,721,345 19s 7d. for a total number of 83,176 slaves and in 1840 there were 1,874 proprietors of whom 940, inclusive of 338 females possessed more than ten acres each.

Six years later sugar was being produced on 491 sugar estates using 506 windmills and one steam engine. Sir Robert Schom-burgk's verdict on the prospects for sugar investors was quite un-like Ligon's glowing prospectus in the golden age. 'The agricultural community', wrote Schomburgk in 1846, 'can only with great exertion and all possible economy earn a modest return for the capital invested in the cultivation of the soil'. Poor prospects were not helped by the disastrous fire which consumed ten acres of Bridgetown in 1845. The worst calamity was experienced in 1854 when 20,000 people died of cholera which was widespread that year. This horror was aggravated by food riots. Another extensive fire in Bridgetown during 1860 piled up the suffering.

Political fires were later kindled when an Irish-born reforming governor, Pope-Hennessy, tried to bulldoze the Barbadians to accept his solutions. His criticism of the island's oligarchs sparked discontent among the negroes who were inflamed to riot. The rioters were suppressed, but Pope-Hennessy was promoted to another British colony. The action of the Barbadian Defence League so impressed the Colonial Office that in 1885 the island was separated from the Windward Islands, of which government it had been the seat for more than 50 years. The separatist political heritage of these years has lasted into modern times.

The hurricane of 1898, in which 100 lives were lost, was the worst since the terrible disaster of 1831 when whole families were buried in ruins, wooden huts were blown down and the barracks and hospitals of St Anne's near the Garrison savannah were made useless and troops forced to live under canvas.

In 1881 an idea proposed by Sir William Colebrooke in 1854

was finally accepted for improving the executive government of Barbados and the Executive Committee was introduced as an embryonic cabinet in miniature. Political progress had dragged on leaden feet during the 100 years which elapsed between the abolition of apprenticeship in 1838 and the outbreak of hunger riots in 1937. The outbreak of war delayed reforms, but the franchise was widened in 1944 and in 1946 the first real step to cabinet government was introduced when Sir Grattan Bushe selected Grantley Adams to initiate government measures in the House of Assembly as spokesman of an Executive Committee of which he and other members of the Barbados Labour Party were members. It was unfortunate that the introduction of party government into Barbados had strong racial overtones. The opponents of the Barbados Labour Party, despite limited support from certain prosperous coloured persons, were fundamentally representatives of white landowners, merchants and the majority of white executives and clerks in Bridgetown. The enfranchisement of all registered persons aged 21 years and over followed in 1951. From that year erosion of white representatives in the House of Assembly continued mercilessly. In the elections preceding independence in November 1966 not a single white member was elected to an Assembly where no coloured man had sat between the years 1639 and 1843. The only one elected since was not born in Barbados.

There was a time in 1897 when it looked as if the mainspring of Barbadian history was about to be shattered and the islanders would have to flee from a place which could no longer feed its population. But Britain that year had in Joseph Chamberlain a Secretary of State who believed that it would be dishonourable for England to forsake the West Indies. He sternly warned the Cabinet of which he was a member that conditions in the West Indies were alarming and almost certain to become disastrous and dangerous in a very short time.

Sugar then accounted for 97% of the exports of Barbados, and its price had fallen more than 50% in 50 years. Chamberlain's masterful prodding of the British Cabinet resulted in abolition of the bounty system which had encouraged European growers of beet at the expense of sugar-cane growers on British plantations. New heart was put into the West Indian sugar planters and

Barbados was made the centre of an Imperial Department of Agriculture whose activities produced an early twentieth-century agricultural revolution throughout the West Indies and spread outwards to other colonial plantations.

Chamberlain had also persuaded the House of Commons that Britain had placed the labouring population of the West Indies where it was and that money spent on their behalf was not to be considered as 'doles' but as 'necessary expenses of Empire'. At the same time he reminded the House that the West Indies were then buying something like £3 million yearly from British manufacturers and that something like 40,000 families in Britain were dependent upon the trade with the West Indian colonies.

Chamberlain's constructive imperialism, the first truly 'constructive' policy that Barbados had experienced since the first settlement, set the islanders on a path which might have altered history had there been no outbreak of war in Europe. So successful had been Britain's encouragement of West Indian agriculture that by 1910 grants in aid were no longer needed by any of the West Indian governments. A new prosperity was developing from the confidence which West Indian planters then placed in the imperial relationship and from the novel direction of educational policies geared to the production of trained workers on the land. Unhappily it was not possible to encourage such attitudes after two World Wars had twice turned the world upside down. When in 1951 all Barbadians of 21 were granted the vote new expectations predominated amongst new electors and agriculture was steadily dethroned as new economic activities like building, light industries, tourism and services appealed to young voters who rejected agriculture and sugar growing as a return to the bad old days of masters and slaves.

Two attempts to achieve West Indian political federation were followed by the establishment of a Caribbean Free Trade Area, but the spirit of 'going it alone' is still as deep rooted as it was when white Barbadians combined against Pope-Hennessy in 1876.

The pattern which will prevail in the West Indies as the twenty-first century approaches is not yet clear and will not perhaps be visible until time proves whether or not the centuries' old European influences will be wholly submerged by new cultural and ideological trends.

Barbados, though technically a sovereign independent nation since November 1966, cannot isolate itself from its past or its present. The British overlord has been expelled as principal ring-leader of the island's dance of political and social life, but the relics of the overlord system remain. The institutions of a white Westernised civilisation, the class distinctions of an oligarchic society, the schools and churches, the courts and police, the sports, manners and pursuits of property owners have continued to be reflected by those who have inherited the legacies bequeathed by Anglicised generations. Nor should anyone be surprised, since adults of 21 and over were enfranchised only as recently as 1951.

In 1922 a visiting British commissioner, the Hon. E. F. Wood, recorded that land and industry in Barbados was almost exclusively in the hands of European large proprietors and that power lay in the House of Assembly which represented only a small electorate with high franchise qualifications. Forty years later power had passed to the representatives of all who were aged 18 or over on election day. The speed of enfranchisement in Barbados was precipitate compared to that of England, where women of 21 did not get the vote until 1926.

Size rather than political sovereignty and advanced suffrages will govern Barbados' future. There are only 116 square miles of land in the entire kingdom on which live a population that despite decades of birth control and extensive emigration rapidly approaches one quarter of a million in number.

Barbados, which is no longer the responsibilty of any external power, has to answer the question whether it can satisfy the requirements of a population which seems destined to want more and more of the good things of life without having rights of access to resources outside its boundaries, or rights of emigration to other countries. What further development is possible and what effect would it have on the environment?

The legacy of continuous economic development elsewhere has been the destruction of the environment and the replacement of 'a natural rhythm' of life by forced rhythms which have perpetually to be adjusted to faster speeds which can produce evils as great or greater than those which they intended to alleviate. Will Barbados, with so little room for manoeuvre, be overwhelmed by such progress?

Already the island has benefited from many refinements of late twentieth century living, but it has also succumbed to some of its modern diseases like galloping inflation, industrial strife, under-employment and similar concomitants of economic expansion. The very rapidity of its political maturity and the comparative inexperience of the men and women who have inherited a fragile economic system devised for slower rotations of growth, may yet distract attention from the overwhelming need for continued migration if its young people of talent are not to be imprisoned on so small an area of the earth's surface. However natural it may be for a human being to love the cradle of its infancy, the instinct to stretch one's wings and fly away from the nest is no less natural for men and women than it is proper for birds, and always worthwhile.

Those who have moulded the destinies of Barbados in the colonial past, those who have led tiny Caribbean islets into paths of independence and steered courses through narrows which lead into wide oceans, all profited in great degree from their experiences of a larger world. Those who follow them as decades of independence roll back into history are more likely to be fashioned by the relatively few paternal acres which they have inherited. Will such men or women astonish the world with some new message?

Perhaps, but it is far more likely that the future of the islands will lie in association with a greatly expanded Caribbean polity and finally with integration into a world where freedom of movement will be acknowledged as the basic right of every man and woman. Time alone will decide. Meanwhile for those who seek temporary escape from far more highly geared civilisations the small size of Barbados, its profusion of beaches, its sunshine and its relatively slow pace of life offer the chief ingredients of a happy holiday, the opportunity to unwind and get closer to Nature, the great mother of men. Those who go to Barbados with such pure intentions are unlikely for a long time to be disappointed in their hopes.

18　*The Barbados Mulatto Girl, by Agostino Brunias (Cunard Gallery)*

II FOREGROUND

19 and 20 (opposite). Above: Hilton Hotel near Bridgetown.
Below: Bridgetown in 1969

F

6 Bridgetown and its Environs

Indians reached Barbados by canoes from Trinidad before Duke William had established his right to England by conquest. When in 1628 Carlisle's Englishmen arrived inside the natural harbour of the island the descendants of the early Indian settlers had either abandoned the island or had been taken away as captives by Spaniards to work in mines of the Spanish American mainland.

According to some historians of Barbados Carlisle's settlers found a bridge and stepping stones which they believed to have been made by Indians, but Ligon writing in 1647 makes no mention of an Indian bridge. He simply said that the Town, which was at the time about the size of Hounslow, had been called the Bridge because a 'long Bridge was made at first over a little nook of the sea, which was rather a bog than a sea'.

The fact that the town was often called Indian-Bridge Town throughout the seventeenth century suggests that Indian workmen had once constructed a bridge. Since Indians were brought to Barbados by Sir William Courteen's representatives in 1627 it is possible that they were the bridge builders.

The town's title varied for decades between 'Indian Bridge' and 'St Michael's'. Both names eventually fell into disuse and by the eighteenth century Bridgetown became the common appellation of the capital city of Barbados, which since 1872 has been provided with two bridges. The most recent of these, the one nearest to the open sea, is still 'swung' from time to time to permit the passage of high-masted ships or motor vessels. Between the 'swing' or Chamberlain bridge, as it was later called in memory of the great Colonial Secretary who saved the West Indian sugar industry, and the Molehead erected in the mid-nineteenth century, the outer Careenage of Bridgetown welcomes vessels of many types. There in the winter months may be seen riding at anchor sleek luxurious yachts proclaiming the names of fashionable Mediterranean ports, schooners and motor vessels from other West Indian islands, deep sea trawlers, gaily painted small fishing boats, tugs, dinghies, sailboats and skiffs. There too you may sometimes see harbour policemen exercise, fully clad in tourist-attracting pinafore-type tunics and wearing broad brimmed straw hats on their heads. The dark blue waters of the Careenage have smoothed the arrivals of many famous men and women to Bridgetown; among them Henry Morgan, George Washington, Rodney, Nelson, Winston Churchill, Queen Elizabeth II and Prince Philip, Princess Margaret and the Prince of Wales, Dr Alain Bombard, Thor Heyerdahl, Aldous Huxley, Sonja Henie, Tommy Steele and thousands more. Others as famous have arrived by air.

The streets which surround the Careenage have often been closed during Royal visits and state occasions and events tinged with joy or sadness. High seas, especially during periodic storms or hurricanes, have often washed up floating debris sucked from the shore and mingled with it rotting bodies of dead fish or animals. Servants, slaves, cattle and other commodities for centuries used to be exposed there for sale just as today inanimate cargoes are still loaded or off-loaded regardless of traffic.

Picturesque, authentically West Indian, international and salty tanged from the sea, the vitality of Bridgetown is to be found in the narrow basin of its Careenage. The best time to be there is after the working day has ended. When the sun sets a short sharp twilight splashes crimson-red gold-flecked blue-backed swathes of colour across the heavens and down upon the heaving ocean before darkness falls, as if poured out of a vast tar barrel, scattering blackness over the lands of the interior.

The archangel Michael, whose name for decades fought that of the Bridge for the right to be the town's appellation, was the first saint to be honoured in a church constructed within city limits. The parish of St Michael still recalls this dedication and the Saint is also invoked at the large Anglican cathedral which is only a few minutes' walk from the city's heart in Trafalgar Square.

It is impossible for the visitor spending a few days in the island to understand the solidity of the English impact upon

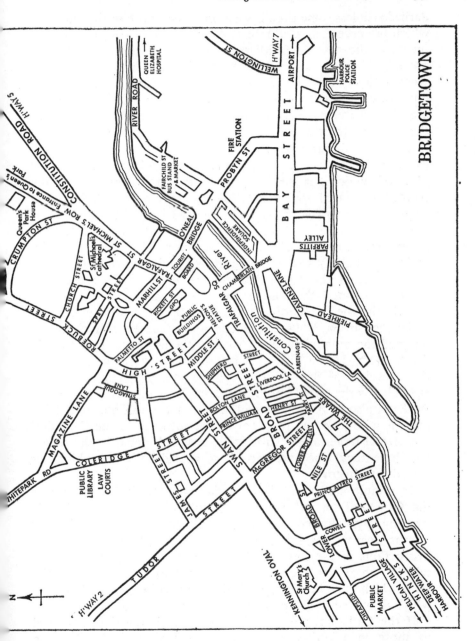

Barbados unless some time is spent in one or more of the churches which preserve dedicated tablets, heraldic crests and other monuments of the past. In St Michael's cathedral several inscriptions proclaim the very sad ends of many English youths whose lives were untimely snuffed by the ravages of the then unknown and unregarded mosquito, carrier of dreaded yellow fever. But there are also several monuments which deserve attention because of the skills of their sculptors.

Of especial interest is one commemorating Robert Hooper, and executed in the style of Grinling Gibbons. Unique because made of wood, which has survived the onslaughts of termites, is the painted memorial to Thomas Duke, Treasurer of Barbados in 1750, and member of a family connected with the Stracheys of England. The Cathedral also boasts in the Braithwaite memorial a very fine work by the British sculptor John Flaxman, who designed regularly for the Wedgwoods and who held the chair of sculpture at the Royal Academy. A pupil of Canova's, John Gibson, executed the simple but elegant memorial to Frances Bovell who died suddenly at 32. John Bacon, whose works are to be seen in St Paul's of London and other English churches, sculpted the monument in St Michael's which records the tragic death of Mrs Letitia Austin. A famous sculptor of monuments in the churches of Bristol and Bath, Wood, also contributed to St Michael's the twin cherub memorial for Katherine Sims Smith. W. Paty, also of Bristol, made the monument to Thomas Griffith and his wife Jane. On the floor at the entrance to the Cathedral are several large tablets still legible although dated in the seventeenth century. They are records of an old Barbados which has passed into history.

To sample modern Barbados today's visitor should stray near the Cathedral on a Sunday afternoon when be-ribboned girls wearing gay coloured cottons and stiff muslin prints, and sober youths wearing ties and dark heavy trousers attend for religious instructions in the heat of the day. Few of the young persons will be white, yet they are Anglicans who have inherited the faith which once belonged exclusively to white men and women who had owned their great grand-parents as chattels or servants.

If the Cathedral still remains the most impressive memorial to those men and women who preserved Barbados for the

Anglican discipline, Sir Richard Westmacott's bronze replica of proud Nelson in Trafalgar Square close by, no longer receives the honour which is due to him as 'preserver' of the West Indies. The traditional laying of a wreath by governor and other high officials on the anniversary of Trafalgar was carried out for the last time on 21 October 1962 and is unlikely ever to take place again. For today's Barbadian does not like to be reminded of the imperial past. He seeks instead heroes among coloured countrymen like those who have already been honoured in names given to new bridges, schools and boulevards. Earlier white Barbadians, who never knew that Nelson in his letters had described their island as 'barbarous' and 'detestable', bought Eggington's Green in Bridgetown, renamed it Trafalgar Square and erected Westmacott's splendid life size tribute there before dawn on 22 March 1813. Dwarfed by the modern Financial Building which provided the central stage for the ceremonial Independence Day Celebrations of 30 November 1966, uncared for by the majority of today's Barbadians, Sir Richard Westmacott's statue of Nelson might be more fittingly removed to the courtyard of the Barbados Museum, which still uniquely preserves in Barbados ways of life which no longer represent the dominant culture patterns of new élites. Meanwhile any visitor who can borrow a pair of good binoculars or who has a good telephoto lens in his camera may profitably examine at close range the remarkable strength and vigour of Nelson's head revealed through the skill and craftmanship of a great English artist in bronze.

Another relic of an older Bridgetown lies below the Financial Building. It is the Mediterranean Dolphin Fountain, which for many decades after its inauguration in 1865 used to refresh the residents of Bridgetown as they took pleasure from the shade trees in the small gardens where today only a single Cannon Ball tree still stands. Nowadays the fountain splashes rarely, as if all its tears for past glory had been shed and it was now dried up.

Since 1872 the House of Assembly and the Upper House or Legislative Council, which evolved into the Senate before independence, always meet in the coral stone buildings across from Trafalgar Square. Stained glass panes in the Assembly Hall depict all the Royal British Sovereigns who ruled over England and

Barbados from the time of James I until Queen Victoria's reign. Oliver Cromwell is shown in a pane, but not his son. James is commemorated because the first visit to Barbados by Englishmen was made shortly before his death in 1625. A small bust on the top of the Assembly's stone steps honours the first coloured Barbadian to become Solicitor General and Chief Justice. He, Sir Conrad Reeves, also enjoyed the rare and posthumous distinction of being the only coloured gentleman to fraternise with white Victorian planters and merchants in a postcard portrait gallery hanging in the exclusive men's Bridgetown Club on the top floor of the Barbados Mutual Building.

A large portrait painting more than 100 years old survives in the small dining-room where today's Assemblymen eat during sessions. It is a likeness of William Murrell Howard, 'father of the Agricultural Societies' which were first formed in the early nineteenth century. He was also captain and adjutant of the St Philip's Regiment of Militia. In the Senate Chamber, in addition to a small marble statue of Puck and an old umbrella rack, are three paintings of interest, one by Giacomo Anicono of Colonel Henry Worsley Governor from 1722–1731, and two portraits of members of the Harewood family. The first is of Edwin Baron Harewood, the second that of the first Earl. A descendant of these Harewoods, the Hon. Gerald Lascelles is a cousin of Queen Elizabeth. He escorted her over his estate at Belle in St Michael when she visited the island shortly before independence.

The Lascelles name is still remembered in Lascelles plantation near Holetown. Henry, from whom the Earls of Harewood are descended, was a merchant and collector of customs in Bridgetown before he became a West Indian merchant in London and Member of Parliament for Northallerton. His son Edwin was first Baron Harewood. This title became extinct on Edwin's death. Edward, the eldest surviving son of Edward Lascelles, Collector of Customs in Barbados, inherited the family properties in England and Barbados, and was created Baron Harewood in 1796 and Viscount Lascelles, Earl of Harewood in 1812. Besides the Mount and Belle plantations members of the Lascelles family previously also owned Lascelles, Thicket, Fortescue and Kent plantations.

The Financial Building, the Duncan O'Neal bridge, Independence Square, the Fairchild market, and the Queen Elizabeth

Hospital, all products of the sixties, have been grafted on, as it were, to the trading and political centre of old Bridgetown. Like the new Barbadian flag they represent the aspirations of new Barbadians who want to build a future for which the European past was but an accidental preparation. Independence meant change and an end to a status of inferiority for the majority. It did not overthrow an establishment. It set up its own standards.

Prince Philip opened the hospital, which was built with the aid of British funds and was fittingly named for the Queen, his wife. Like the deepwater harbour and the modern government buildings in Bay Street this 600-bed hospital marked happy years of co-operation between men in London and Sir Grantley Adams' 'liberal' socialist administration which was enabled through British development funds to do what no previous government of Barbados could have done without such financial help.

The lead given by government in the erection of modern Barbadian buildings was soon followed by banks and large commercial enterprises in Bridgetown, where since independence workmen ceaselessly alter, demolish, renew or construct. Six banks now have headquarters in Bridgetown and many branches in other parts of the island.

The principal narrow street, which was named Broad for some long-forgotten reason, has been gradually transformed from a street of general-purpose stores into the major banking centre of the City. Extensive fires in the late 'sixties have helped on the construction of other modern buildings. The old Ideal Store was lamented as an architectural loss but has been replaced by one more in harmony with the rest of the street. The new Trident House and the Barbados Mutual Building in Lower Broad Street indicate how older colonial patterns were blended to suit modern needs and by the twenty-first century may come to be regarded as symptomatic of the new style of a period, just as the Da Costa Building has perpetuated mid-Victorian tastes into the latter half of the twentieth century.

Commercial and banking Bridgetown come to an abrupt halt at the bus stop and car park which separate the Air Canada building from the ancient wood-galleried and stone building at the corner of Cheapside, where Mayor, Aldermen and Councillors briefly guided the City's government until it was engulfed and directed by the central administration.

The buses which ply from Bridgetown to the North are open on both sides and are painted bright reds and yellows. They come and go at intervals, manoeuvring their way delicately in and out of groups of women carrying loaded trays balanced by cloth pads upon their heads. Other women in the bus park squat open legged on small portable wooden benches. They tempt passers-by with popcorn, coconut cakes, peanuts, fruit and other wares of proven popular appeal. The car park is a favourite resort of the open air barber who shears heads under spreading evergreen trees. Beloved for their shade, these trees at Christmastide attract choirs from all over the island. Then clusters of coloured bulbs are strung around their limbs. Sometimes domino players set up their boards under the evergreens. Or you may see a group of 'warri' players who move horse nickers from hole to hole of heavy gouged wood, perpetuating a game brought to Barbados from Africa.

Open-air selling is slowly disappearing from city streets as formal markets have been established on either side of the main approaches to Bridgetown, at Fairchild Street to the south and at Cheapside to the north. Roofed over, these markets protect both those who sell and those who buy from rain or sun. They are well stocked with home-grown vegetables, fruit and 'ground provisions' such as potatoes, yams or eddoes.

The visitor who goes to the Cheapside market on foot will perhaps have spared a few moments to look at the City Church of St Mary's which was consecrated in 1827, having been dedicated by William Coleridge, the first Bishop of the Caribbees, to the Blessed Virgin Mary on 22 July 1825. Its glory passed with the decay in the 'forties of Fontabelle as a fashionable residential suburb north of the city.

In May 1631 the Churchyard around St Mary's was the site of the judicial murder of Sir William Tufton, an early governor.

Pelican Village behind Cheapside market on the sea lies half way between the centre of Bridgetown and the modern deep water harbour. It is a modern complex of small shops constructed on land reclaimed between the former Pelican or Bird Island and the shore of Fontabelle. Designed by Robertson Ward Associates,

architects of Sandy Lane Hotel and of other magnificent private
and public buildings erected during the 'sixties, Pelican Village
is designed for the convenience and comfort of visitors. Island
crafts, souvenirs, paintings, corals, algae and other products of
the sea are offered for sale in attractive shops which stock a
variety of other 'tourist' merchandise. Fanned by the sea breezes,
the restaurant offers good food and drinks modestly priced and
caters for residents as well as visitors.

Those who drive in from the north might like to park their
cars at Pelican Village and walk into the city from there. Behind
Pelican Village is a modern handicraft centre and to the north
of it a small industrial park provided by government for approved
manufacturers on tax holidays. The Samuel Jackman Prescod
Technical School is further to the north just outside the precincts
of the enclosed harbour. Inside the harbour area, the yield of
Barbados' sugar-cane fields is stored and piped annually from a
huge pyramid-shaped building directly into the holds of steam-
ships which carry raw sugar in bulk to English ports. Adjoining
the Institute, which received technical assistance in its early
days from West Germany, is an open area used for tennis tournaments, dog shows and other sports or social events. The Barbados
College of the University of the West Indies was located there
before it moved to its present delightful quarters on Cave Hill.

Visitors who arrive in Barbados by air have no idea of the
cleanliness of the deep water harbour. An enormous boon to the
island's economy, the harbour by 1971 had become too small for
the needs of an expanding economy.

The headquarters of Esso in Barbados now occupies the site
of an old Barbadian mansion, Holborn, which was the seat of
seventeenth-century governors. Esso's courtyard is the starting
point of the Annual June Rally which the company promotes
and which is organised by the Rally Club of Barbados.

The Esso service station is obliquely opposite to Barbados'
most famous cricket ground at Kensington Oval where the giants
of world cricket entertain many thousands of fans, some of
whom climb into tree tops and watch from roofs and walls if
they cannot or do not want to pay admission fees. Cricket, not
sugar, is king in Barbados, and will endure longer. Those who do
not worship at the shrine of cricket will always be less honoured

there than those who do, visitors always excepted. The famous Oval ground is not remarkable in any way and is used for football and other sports. Before the opening of the modern sports stadium by the Prince of Wales in 1970 athletics and bicycle racing also took place at the Oval.

Like St Mary's the Church of St Leonard's behind the Oval in Westbury Road is a reminder of a Barbadian way of life which is as dead and buried as the men and women whose English birthplaces still peep at you from ancient moss-covered tombstones.

It is possible to reach Swan Street by walking through the large department store of Da Costa's, the Selfridges of Bridgetown. Until recently this street, once known as Jew Street because of the number of Jewish families who lived there, retained many of the upper balconies common to city dwellings. Some still survive in Swan Street, Tudor Street, Baxters Road and Roebuck Street. As early as 1680 civil rights had been extended to Jews in Barbados, when their testimony was admitted in all civil suits. An act of 1831 removed all restraint or disabilities still imposed upon Jews. In Magazine Lane an old Jewis cemetery near to the former synagogue records the names of many Jewish families who made Barbados their home between the mid-seventeenth and early eighteenth century. Jews once had no less than five burial grounds on the island.

The Montefiore fountain, with its solemn warning 'Look to the End', preserves an association with one of British Jewry's best known families. It faces the Carnegie Library and the Law Courts and is near to the synagogue. Once it stood at the lower end of Broad Street where its water refreshed 'cabbies' before they were finally replaced by taxi drivers in the 'forties of this century. In 1920 the synagogue building was sold following dispersal of the congregation overseas. During the 'thirties and 'forties other Jewish families found asylum in Barbados. Some of these have put down roots and visitors may attend religious services on Friday evenings at True Blue, Rockley New Road.

The edifice of the synagogue, which was consecrated on the 20 March 1838, remains. It has distinctive, lancet-shaped windows. The interior was formerly paved in alternate squares of black and white marble and the ceiling was chastely painted in relief. A marble fountain from the courtyard now stands at the entrance to the Barbados Museum, where the synagogue's large ornamental clock and Candle lamp for the Festival of Lights are also prominently preserved for posterity.

The coral stone Library, a gift to Barbados from Andrew Carnegie, was opened in 1906. It replaced the first free library of 1847 and incorporated the libraries of the Literary and Clerical Societies.

The Law Courts adjoining mark the site of the Town Hall, where the Legislature met from 1729 to 1784 over the Town Gaol. Coleridge in 1825 pilloried an arrangement whereby 'His Majesties Council, the General Assembly, the Judges, the Juries, the Debtors and the Felons all lived together in the same house. . . . House of Lords, St Stephen's, Westminster Hall, Newgate and Marshalsea, all in one.' The felons were removed in 1846 to a palatial Glendairy prison overlooking 'Condemned Road', but debtors continued to be held in the Town Gaol until 1875. John Pope-Hennessy, the newly arrived governor, paid 18 shillings to set a screaming debtor free and later by public proclamation ordered the prison to be closed, a humanitarian act for which he has not been remembered with sufficient gratitude by later generations. Pope-Hennessy did not please the oligarchs of the day. They resented his attempt to make more acceptable their political power through appointments to his Executive Council of the Colonial Secretary, the Attorney General, the Officer in Command of the Troops and the solitary liberal Barbadian planter, Sir Graham Briggs.

Beyond St Michael's Cathedral to the south of Trafalgar Square are the two major schools of Barbados: Harrison College for boys, Queen's College for girls. They lie on either side of Queen's Park. Harrison College was formerly housed in the Masonic building which still stands behind St Michael's Cathedral.

In his autobiography, Leigh Hunt tells how his grandfather, who was rector of St Michael's, recommended William Lauder a 'Tory' sympathiser and friend of Dr Samuel Johnson to the mastership of the free school in the eighteenth century. Lauder failed to give satisfaction as a teacher of Latin and set up a huckster's shop with the aid of an African lady whom he bought. The daughter of the huckster by Lauder grew up to be the most famous landlady in Barbadian history. She obtained £700 from Prince William Henry, the future William IV, for a furniture smashing frolic which he conducted with the aid of officers from the 49th Regiment. The incident occurred in 1786 when the Prince was serving on the *Pegasus*. The landlady, Rachel Pringle Polgreen, whose huge bulk is preserved in a caricature painting by Rowlandson, spent her Royal windfall on improvements to the hostelry which she called the Royal Navy Hotel. Long before the age of image makers Rachel was adept in the art of public relations. Running hotels or taverns was a sure way of gaining popularity in a slave-owning society.

Girls employed in taverns could even buy their freedom through sale of their favours to guests. The army doctor, George Pinckard, described Bridgetown's tavern girls in 1796 as 'of erect figure and stately carriage . . . without shoes and stockings, in a short white jacket and a thin short petticoat . . . a white turban on the head . . . neck and shoulders left bare'. Service left much to be desired at table. Pinckard complained that there were too many servants: 'badly regulated . . . each being idle and inactive, waiting for another to step before him when any thing is called for, and although you have a crowd of servants round you, it is difficult to obtain what you want.' Unlike today's hotels, most of the taverns in the eighteenth and nineteenth century were in Bridgetown. They took their name from the tavern keeper. Some of the most famous of these were Nancy Clarke, Mary Bella Green, Betsy Lemon, Sabina Brade, Rachel Pringle Polgreen, Betty Austin, Caroline Lee (who gave her name to a yellow sweet potato) and Hannah Lewis. The most famous of Bridgetown's hotels, the Ice House, disappeared when the coral stone edifice of the modern Bank of Nova Scotia replaced it in the 'sixties.

Ice first came to Barbados in the year of Queen Victoria's accession. The Ice House Hotel owed its success to the enterprise of Dudley Page Cotton, a native of New Hampshire. He was director of two West Indian importing firms, D. P. Cotton and Co. of Barbados and C. L. Haley and Co. of Trinidad, and he was also a director of the Boston-based exporting firm of Messrs. Cotton and Haley. Ice was at first delivered to buyers at the Ice House on the pierhead before there was a merger with Mrs

Roach's hotel. Association was completed by 1846, the year when Dudley Page Cotton married Rebecca Jane, the youngest daughter of the late Nathaniel Roach.

Few places in Barbados have ever excited the pens of visiting writers more than the Ice House. Trollope first put it on the map when he described how he was introduced there to 'cocktail, with which I had to make closer acquaintance afterwards, cocktail being the established corrective of West Indian languor, without which life is impossible'.

The Ice House is no more, but cocktail in various forms remains the solace of all who thirst in Barbados. In the quiet recesses of the Bridgetown Club it still fills with joy those who agree with Bertie Wooster that in 'certain fundamentals of life the West Indians are ahead of our own European civilisation. . . .' To justify his claim Bertie gives green swizzle as an example of cocktail. The chief ingredients are white rum, falernum and a sprig of wild worm bush. The effect of these smooth little cocktails on Bertie was inspiring. In the *Rummy Affair of Old Biffy*, Bertie promises that if he were ever to marry and have a son 'Green Swizzle Wooster is the name that will go down on the register'. No other writer has praised West Indian cocktails more ardently than Wodehouse in this story, but Trollope was the first author to set a fashion for cocktails after his experience in the Ice House of Bridgetown.

Harrison College, which commemorates the memory of the Churchwarden of St Michael's who started the free school behind the cathedral in 1733, took on a new dimension when it opened on its present site in 1871. Mangrove Lodge, the headmaster's residence, still retains a flavour of the Victorian age as do some of the older coral stone buildings.

Queen's House, in the park which surrounds Harrison College and the Department of Agriculture, was the stately residence of the General commanding British forces in the East Caribbean until 1906. Lady Gilbert Carter, supported by public-spirited citizens of Barbados, was responsible for the transformation of house and grounds into a place of refreshment and beauty where citizens could take pride in lake, terraces, pavilions, bandstand, lawns, bowers, avenues of gaily flowering shrubs, vines and thick leaved shade trees. The glory that was Queen's Park gradually receded to meet the needs of more clamorous social services and recreations and Queen's House grew tattier every year until Oliver Messel, the famous theatrical designer and amateur architect, offered his services as restorer in the 'seventies. For decades the grounds of the Park have been used for exhibitions, trade fairs, political meetings and religious festivals while the open grass-covered fields serve in turn the needs of footballers, cricketers, motorcyclists and horse riders, or make a handy circus for the judging of prize cattle.

Queen's College, which will achieve its hundredth birthday in 1983, accommodated nearly 500 girls in 1973. In the 'fifties it swallowed up the grounds of the old Combermere Boys' School and later won new playing fields from the canalised Constitution River. Its buildings stand boldly looking across at the decayed splendour of the residence of former upholders of Empire. It is a proud institution which prepares girls of the new Barbados to fulfil future roles as mothers and leaders. Since women outnumber men in Barbados Queen's College is likely to become more significant year by year.

Constitution Road, which divides Queen's Park from Queen's College, leads directly to Government House which crowns a hill overlooking the once fashionable and beautiful suburb of Belleville. Despite heavy losses caused by the hurricane of 1955 the towering cabbage palm trees of Belleville and the well-kept gardens of spacious villas recall the heyday of Barbadian respectability when Belleville, Strathclyde, Fontabelle, the public gardens and fountains of Bridgetown, the Esplanade and the Rocks, Queen's Park and many private mansions and stately homes around and near the city reflected British pride in property.

A few of these mansions of Edwardian Barbados survive today as institutions serving the people of Barbados. Notable amongst them are Erdiston on the Pine, Enmore and the Ursuline Convent in Collymore Rock and Grassfield House, site of St Michael's Girls' School, near to the Queen Elizabeth Hospital. Pilgrim, an 18-acre estate on which the modern Government House stands, was leased in 1702 as the seat of the island's Governor and commanded in chief. Sir Bevil Granville, the first Governor to take up residence there, was shot at from the road,

21 (*opposite*) *Sir Richard Westmacott's bronze statue of 'Nelson, preserver of the West Indies' Trafalgar Square, Bridgetown*

before today's high wall had been constructed. His successor, the unpopular Mr Mitford Crowe, found 18 acres too small and infertile for his horses so additional lands were secured. After £2000 had been spent on improving home and gardens the whole property was bought in 1734 for £1345. A self-styled 'architect' governor, Sir Thomas Robinson, made extensive alterations, including a portico between 1742 and 1747. He was lucky to obtain the Assembly's sanction for this expenditure, but he had to pay from his own pocket the then enormous sum of £4,200 which, without Assembly approval, he had spent on erecting the best armoury in the West Indies for the defence of Barbados.

Today's Government House, except for minor alterations, was constructed according to plans put forward by an architect James Howard in March 1755. It suffered extensive damage in the great hurricane of 1780 when the armoury was destroyed. Further damage to the roof and other parts of the building was caused by the hurricanes of 1831 and 1891. Governor Ricketts, a Jamaican who governed Barbados from 1794 to 1800, installed his mulatto mistress from Tobago at Pilgrim, where she enjoyed all a wife's privileges except the honour of presiding at public dinners. It was during Ricketts' term of office that Barbados freely contributed about £13,000 to the British government to help pay for the war against Napoleon's France.

Now and at all times the heart of Barbadian social life, Government House and its beautiful gardens may be seen by visitors on special open days. Occasionally it may also be seen as the setting for a ball or other evening function which has been organised in aid of local charities. Unlike the year 1879, when two Royal Princes Albert Victor and George of Wales attended a ball there and noted 'not one black face in all the rooms', today's social occasions reflect the new society when everyone expects a black or mulatto Minister to lead a Royal Princess on to the floor.

St Anne's Castle on the sea, headquarters of the Barbados Regiment, looks on to a 50-acre open Savannah which is a traditional ceremonial parade ground, and major open recreational centre on the southern outskirts of Bridgetown. Site of the historic hauling down of the British flag at midnight of 29 November 1966 the Savannah has also witnessed many an im-

22 *and* 23 *(opposite) Above: Codrington College, St John. Below: Water police patrolling Bridgetown's inner harbour as it was in the 1950s*

G

pressive ceremony under the Empire and continues to be used for horse races, rugby, goat racing, kite-flying, football, cricket and other traditional Barbadian sports. Pavilions and paddocks are maintained there by the Barbados Turf Club whose members stage three or four race meetings yearly.

Surrounding the Savannah are buildings and monuments which recall the presence of British regiments in Barbados from the late seventeenth century until the first decade of the twentieth century. The Drill Hall and Armoury, the Iron Barracks, the Officers' and Sergeants' Married Quarters, the Military hospital, the Military Prison and the old Guard room and Clock Tower have all survived to the present day and are used for a variety of purposes.

The Engineers' Pier is still serviceable and is an integral part of the modern Holiday Inn on the sea. Opposite and to the left of the government-owned Hilton Hotel is the military cemetery where the young Prince of Wales who became King George V led a funeral party from the *Bacchante* at the burial of James Sims, naval schoolmaster.

Close to the Turf Club paddocks the Barbados Museum occupies the site of the Military Prison whose spiked railings and small wicket gate vividly recall the building's original function. A prisoner's cell has been reconstructed inside to remind visitors of the rigours of army punishment not so long ago. The building was erected by military engineers in 1853. The late Eustace Maxwell Shilstone, a former clerk of the House of Assembly and successful solicitor, was largely responsible for the foundation of the Museum in 1933 as a department of the Barbados Museum and Historical Society. Under the late Neville Connell, barrister-at-law and historian, the Museum expanded greatly in the years between 1945 and his untimely death in 1973. The Jubilee Gallery, which commemorates the silver jubilee of King George V, contains the Museum's first collection of shells and specimens and maps of the island's geological structure. It also has interesting mementoes of the tragic eruption of Mt. Pelée in 1902, when the Paris of the West Indies, St Pierre in Martinique, was covered with burning lava. Dust from St Vincent's volcano, The Soufrière, is also preserved. Early Amerindian pottery, and tools discovered in Barbados and neighbouring islands illustrate the simple life of the people who inhabited the island before the European invasion.

Other exhibits show the birds, fish and forest trees of the island. Of special interest is the Coronation Gallery, where hundreds of pieces of late eighteenth century glass, snuff boxes, china, silver and rare furniture tell of the period of gracious living which is described by Labat and other writers. The air-conditioned gallery holds West Indian prints bequeathed to the Museum by the late Sir Edward Cunard.

A diorama in the Harewood gallery shows the coral reefs of Barbados and the marine life around them. The Drax gallery is named after a pioneer of sugar growing in the seventeenth century and has specimens of articles once used in the manufacture and transport of sugar. The excellent dioramas in the children's gallery give a quick historical résumé of Barbados from the earliest days of settlement till the late nineteenth century. It forms a fitting memorial of Neville Connell, whose knowledge of art and appreciation of history saved the Barbados Museum from becoming a place in which to preserve relics of the past and gave it a relevance for people of this and future generations.

7 The Gold and Platinum West Coast

The glory of Barbados today is its West Coast. Where 40 years ago manchineel and white wood groves threw shade and leaves on to virgin sandy beaches, today coral stone villas, swimming pools, tropical gardens, private houses, restaurants, beach hotels, boutiques and settler colonies dot a landscape which twists and turns around sandy coves and sandy beaches. Looking down on this coastline from the air between Harrison Point, the most westerly part of Barbados and Paradise Beach, the nearest beach resort to Bridgetown, it is easy to understand why the islanders distinguish the plush villa-speckled northern part of the West Coast with the name of platinum, the rare metal, while gold is used to describe its commercialised and more densely settled areas between Holetown and Bridgetown. The Platinum Coast is where the millionaires live in the winter, the Gold Coast is for the well heeled all the year round.

Until the mid-thirties Freshwater Beach, the site of today's popular Paradise Beach resort, was standing wood down to the water line, where bubbling fresh water springs used to add cool sub-layers to the translucent sea. Boys on bicycles leaving Lands End in Fontabelle used to cross the Indian River by stepping stones and follow a sandy path through Brighton past the West Indian Rum Refinery to reach Freshwater Bay in half an hour. There behind bushes they would strip themselves naked and plunge headlong into the sea without fear of being seen by anyone.

That was 40 years ago. Today there has been a transformation of the simple paradise.

Change began in the late 'twenties when the owner of Walmer Lodge plantation, Burton Ward, decided to build a club house with dance floor and rented bungalows at Freshwater Bay. From such a modest beginning today's fun-hotel Paradise Beach grew up to become after World War Two the leading first beach resort on the West Coast.

Fear of tidal waves or maybe fear of humid summer heat without benefit of the 'trades', 'those winds of God' which always blow most strongly on the Atlantic facing East Coast, kept Barbadians for centuries from building on the sand acres of the splendid West Coast. Distance from the centre was another reason. Motor cars did not become common until the forties although the first Model T Ford reached Bridgetown in 1909, and the first motor omnibus company was registered in 1906. Barbados enjoyed a tradition of always being ten years behind the big world outside and the double mule drawn tram cars ran there until the late 'twenties. Cabbies still plied from under the ever-green fig trees in Trafalgar Square late in the 'forties.

Because sugar used to be loaded direct on to steamers at Six Men's Bay for export overseas and because there was a regular service of schooners or 'droghers' plying between that port and Bridgetown, the building of a highway between the north and Bridgetown did not become important until the century was well advanced. Developments since the 'sixties accordingly require continuous widening of the main coastal road, which now carries so much traffic between 4 and 5 p.m. on working days that wary drivers use the ridge road by way of Cave and Holders Hills or the by-pass round Warrens to Holetown.

Between Freshwater Bay and Batts Rock Bay until the 'thirties stood ruins of a gun emplacement, one of many defensive structures which ringed the West Coast between Carlisle Bay and Maycock's Bay in the north. Retrieved cannons from these old fortifications have been polished up and do duty outside public buildings or stand sentinels in the private gardens of wealthy winter residents.

Looking on to the sky-blue sea off Batts Rock is a high-walled Lazar-house whose gardens once were the final haunts of sufferers from a dread disease long rare in Barbados. Built at a time when leprosy was still common the Lazaretto buildings contain most of the archives of Barbados. The first radio station set up by the government operated from the Lazaretto, and its antenna still dominates the land behind.

Higher up on Cave Hill is the modern campus of the Barbados

College of the University of the West Indies. The Canadian government provided the residential centre for students from other West Indian Islands, while the British government contributed most of the cost of the other buildings. Through the library windows students get a magnificent view of the harbour and of the sea beyond Paradise Beach. The Faculty of Law of the University is located in the grounds at Cave Hill. Within the University complex lies buried the great West Indian cricketer Sir Frank Worrell, a Barbadian who was warden of a college of the University at Mona, Jamaica, when he died in his early forties.

The road which leads up to the University College continues toward the Multi-Racial Centre of the University of Sussex. The road on the left at the end of the University enclave passes by the offices of the World Meteorological Station and continues down to Holders Polo ground, which lies on the outskirts of a converted old Barbadian mansion, refashioned in the 'sixties for a new owner, the Hon. Janet Kidd, daughter of the late Baron Beaverbrook. Mrs Kidd's love of horses found a ready response among the horse-riding plantation community of Barbados, so the field behind the grounds of her mahogany wood is used each year for international show jumping competitions in which her son John frequently takes part. The Barbados Polo Club hold yearly tournaments and play matches against visiting teams from abroad.

At the foot of Holders' Hill is Tamarind Cove, one of a group of four resort hotels operated for a Canadian owner who also has hotels in Edmonton, Vancouver and Bermuda. One of them, Coconut Creek, was built on the site of a popular night-club where Harry Belafonte first sang 'Island in The Sun' for an invited audience and where Joan Collins danced the limbo. Discovery Bay Inn, close to the site of the first British settlement, and Colony Club, the first of the luxury hotels on the Platinum Coast, complete this Canadian hotel chain.

Between Paradise Beach and Coconut Creek is the Village complex of villa-style apartments, landscaped on an escarpment running down to a beach. The Village is under the management of Trust Houses Forte International, who also own and manage the magnificent Sandy Lane Hotel designed by Robertson Ward

Associates and built around standing wood which breasts onto the loveliest curving beach to be found in the Caribbean. A great feature of Sandy Lane Hotel is a circular outdoor dance floor positioned in the dead centre of a natural amphitheatre made of mahogany trees. On moonlit nights the 'winds of God' blow freely and dancing there is a pleasure unobtainable in cities.

The West Coast hotels no longer need the winds of God in summer to cool the bedrooms, dining-rooms or other public rooms. Excellent air conditioning systems regulate the climate indoors. On summer days there is fun to be found on a tranquil sea while the island is aflame with flowering trees.

Behind Sandy Lane a scenic golf course has been landscaped on several levels of rising ground. There concealed among mahogany groves, casuarinas and other shade trees a golfer can discover several of the most attractive 'winter homes' on the island.

On the beach at the extreme left of the Sandy Lane Hotel lies Heronetta, a coral stone mansion jointly owned by Lord Kindersley and Mr Henry Breck of New York. It is a queen among Barbadian modern beach houses, taking second place only to the massive Palladian-style villa of Mr Ronald Tree which stands cheek by jowl to the Colony Club on one side and on the other is flanked by a veritable little jewel of a guest cottage named from its colour the Pink Cottage. Ronald Tree, a banker, former Tory MP and inheritor of a great American fortune, went to Barbados some years after Sir Edward Cunard and Commander Carlyon Bellairs had blazed a trail by building beach houses on the deserted sand acres of the West Coast. Sir Edward put up a splendid Italianate villa which was later acquired by the Marquess of Normanby. The grounds were large enough for a second coral stone house to be built on the water's edge. Commander Bellairs' home Sandacres was converted recently into a beach bar for the flourishing Coral Reef Hotel whose main building Manzinilla was once the private home of the English naval commander who developed Coral Reef in partnership with Victor Marson and Donald Scott.

The West Coast settlers after World War Two brought to Barbados new standards of taste in architecture, furniture and gracious living. Their demand for coral stone homes, hand-made furniture, local paintings, pottery, metal grille tables and chairs encouraged skills which had lain dormant for lack of patronage.

Ronald Tree's great coral stone mansion on Heron Beach is perhaps the most spectacular home Barbados saw since Sam Lord erected the turreted castle on the South East Coast in 1826. Standing on 19 acres of land at Heron Beach the Tree house was designed by a British architect, Geoffrey Jellicoe, to satisfy the owner's concept of the Barbadian equivalent of a Palladian-style villa. On the land side a towering iron gate recalls the magnificent railings in front of Buckingham Palace in London, though there are no guards on duty and anyone can walk freely through the Tree property without discovering wall or barricade. Heron Beach house was completed in 1947 but the lofty avenue of casuarinas or 'miletrees' which lead up to its entrance were planted earlier in 1920. A great lover of trees and gardens, Mr Tree did not disturb the magnificent manchineels which screen the residents of Heron Beach from the sun's glare or the eyes of countless peeping Toms and Janes who walk along the beach. No house in Barbados has sheltered so many internationally famous men and women as guests of Ronald Tree and his wife Marietta; among them have been Sir Winston and Lady Churchill, Adlai Stevenson, the Duke of Devonshire, the Duke of Norfolk, the Earl and Countess of Avon, Aristotle Onassis, the Queen and Prince Philip and David Bailey.

Until Sandy Lane estate was developed in the 'sixties only Mill Reef Club in Antigua had been the preferred winter resort of wealthy Americans in the East Caribbean. Ever since, wealthy Americans have been building homes and becoming good neighbours of wealthy English winter settlers who preceded them to the island. The presence of internationally famous men and women who own modern landscaped homes designed by architects encourages influx of their friends to resort hotels in St James and St Peter every winter. For years the clubs at Coral Reef, Colony and Miramar stood apart as the places for the elegant, rich and fashionable to stay. Coral Reef still attracts every winter a percentage of such people who come to enjoy each other's company or to visit friends at nearby Settlers Beach or Sandpiper Inn.

Gradually the exclusive cottage colonies on the West Coast

are being transformed into luxury hotels as more rooms are needed for more visitors every year. The distinctive cottage colony-type of resort hotel which once made the Platinum Coast of Barbados unique among Caribbean resorts is gradually being replaced by commercial hotels whose managers are responsible to shareholders overseas. The intimate friendliness between well-heeled guests and well-tipped hotel worker is yielding to economic pressures of a hotel industry in which trade union leaders negotiate wages and managers have continuously to recruit and train new staff.

While the West Coast hotels become more commercialised each year new resort complexes have been designed to satisfy less exalted personages who seek golden sunshine all year round. Outstanding among these resorts on the West Coast is the Sunset Crest development of Holetown, where smart hotels and bungalow-type houses have been constructed around a small village with supermarket and service shops. Sunset Crest has a special appeal for Canadians, who are flown in by frequent charter flights from Toronto. Beginning at sea level the development has already spread upwards to the ridge above. Not since the eighteenth century has Holetown seen such activity. Only then the emphasis was on defence, when Barbadians guarded the bay with a fort mounted with 28 guns reinforced at St James' church by another battery of 8 guns!

A Barbadian legend subsequently disproved by historians continues to be perpetuated on the Holetown monument facing Sunset Crest. There a plinth wrongly records that Englishmen first landed near that spot in the year 1605. The mistake derived from an interpolation in Purchas' *Pilgrims* to the effect that Englishmen from the ship *Olive Branch* had landed at Barbados in 1605 on their way to St Lucia. The author of *An Houre Glasse of Indian Newes*, John Nicholls, whom Purchas quotes as authority for this statement, in fact made no reference to Barbados when he wrote in 1607. Some day perhaps the authorities in Barbados will add a note to the monument in Holetown recording that the first landing was in fact made in 1625! No correction of dates will however dim the memory of the great celebrations of 20 November 1905 when the issue of an 'Olive Blossom' stamp, a state procession to the Savannah, the erection of a cross at

Indian River, a Stag Breakfast provided by the Speaker and House of Assembly were worthy preliminaries to the laying of the foundation stone on the monolith at Holetown and the regatta which followed in Holetown Bay.

The bell of St James' Church asks God to 'bless King William' in 1696; its font dates back to 1684 and there are some fine examples of the work of British sculptors on the walls. One by W. Lancashire of Bath commemorates two wives of Sir John Gay Alleyne and his son John who died when only 13. The panel of this monument shows a distant prospect of Eton College, England's best-known public school. Another specimen of Lancashire's work, the Hubbard memorial, may be seen in St Peter's Church, Speightstown.

Close to the parish church of St James is the Bellairs Research Institute of McGill University, named after a former British Member of Parliament the late Commander C. W. Bellairs, who first visited Barbados as a young boy on a British warship and later built Sandacres as a retirement home for himself and his American-born wife in 1936. Before his death Commander Bellairs bequeathed his land and Sandacres property to McGill. Dr John Lewis became the first director of the Institute in 1955. Later it was expanded to undertake other projects which were made possible by the Brace bequest. Originally operations were concerned only with tropical biology in the sea, and important studies were made of the sea-egg (urchin), flying fish and local plankton. After the Brace bequest important research was made on the potential of wind power as a generator of electricity, and the use of solar heat for cooking in underdeveloped countries. Other research has been devoted to the study of tropical climatology and to the application of purified salt or brackish water for agricultural purposes in dry soils.

Opposite the entrance to Heron Beach and Colony Club is Porters, one of the best-preserved Barbadian great houses. It belongs to the Hon. Murtogh Guinness, who modernised the swimming pool soon after purchase and erected a small Greek temple approached by double stone steps at the far end of the garden. Porters was at one time the residence of the Director General of the British Company which was approved by Spain in 1713 as the official supplier of African slaves to South

America. A Latin inscription records that the swimming pool was first built by the Director General Dudley Woodbridge in 1735 because of 'constant flooding'. Porters has a long, wooded, winding drive which completely obscures the house from the road. This drive is linked with one of the many 'ghost' stories which the long-stay visitor is likely to hear in Barbados. It is recorded that a certain Henry Alleyne who once lived at Porters was accustomed to drive his pony and trap like a modern Jehu in his anxiety to reach his stately house every evening. It came to pass that the steamer *Amazon* in which he was coming home to Barbados after a journey overseas caught fire at sea and Henry Alleyne never reached the shores of his homeland. His spirit however had one last ride! For on the night of his death his servants at Porters ran out of the front door to see a horse-drawn gig clattering up the drive at fearful speed. They were about to welcome their master back home with shouts of joy when horse and gig vanished in front of their eyes.

A more jolly ghost story is told of Westmorland plantation, which used to belong to a family of Gibsons who emigrated to South Carolina at the beginning of the nineteenth century. In 1911 new residents of Westmorland were entertaining some friends at a typical Barbadian banquet when one guest proposed a toast to the 'old fellow who is buried beneath us'. The toast was drunk quite happily because everyone around the table knew that members of the Gibson family had been buried on the plantation in accordance with usual practice throughout the island. The toast was hardly drunk however when another gentleman at table called for glasses to be filled once more and said 'let us drink his health again'. To show his appreciation the 'old fellow' who was buried beneath them obligingly rapped on the floor above!

Yet another old Barbadian mansion said to be 'haunted' is Alleyndale Hall, a striking Barbadian country home located on the outskirts of Speightstown on the road between Mile and a Quarter and St Lucy's Church. There a clergyman named William Tyrell once cut his throat; he was put in a lead coffin and was buried in the wall of the cellar underneath the house. According to local tradition the ghost of William Tyrell has been known to walk upstairs and leave doors open. The present owners have never experienced his presence. Alleyndale Hall once received a visit from Prince William Henry, wrecker of the Royal Naval Hotel in Bridgetown. The house is named for Sir Reynold Alleyne, baronet, who seems to have been almost as eccentric as Samuel Hall Lord. Why else should he have attempted to ride a horse upstairs at St Nicholas Abbey?

Beyond Porters on the seaside Miramar hotel was once a private beach house owned by Barbados' most successful hotelier, Victor Marson, whose hill house at Highclere looks down from a thousand feet on to the rugged East Coast. After many years of success with the Ocean View hotel on the South Coast Victor Marson was a partner in the launching of the Coral Reef and later converted the Miramar into a small exclusive resort. The Miramar under his management was used for a dinner sequence in the 20th Century Fox film *Island in the Sun*. All the stars of this film, including Dorothy Dandridge and Harry Belafonte, stayed at Coral Reef. The beautiful flowering trees to be seen at Miramar and the avenue of cabbage palms were planted by Victor Marson. A little beyond Miramar on the seaside Maddox, a simple Barbadian house, was converted by Oliver Messel into a place for 'indoor-outdoor living', with porches, upper veranda, lower veranda, and dining-room facing outwards to the sea across thick foliaged screens of tropical trees and ornamental plants.

Several homes of settlers on this coast have been landscaped or remodelled by Oliver Messel and one at the foot of a hill a few hundred yards from Maddox was built according to his special design. Maddox is sometimes open in aid of local charities. It is perhaps the most interesting of all Barbadian homes, if not the most beautiful, because it carries the imprint of the lover of natural beauty who knew how to enhance it with the techniques of the portrait painter and stage designer.

Not far away from Gibbs Beach is the small house where Sir Edward Cunard was living at the time of his death. Gibbs Beach is visible from the road but still retains those quiet charms which once were common to all West Coast beaches between Six Men's Bay and Freshwater.

Above Gibbs Beach on the ridge above is the modern Eastry House, a hotel landscaped around tropical gardens and a large swimming pool. Facing Eastry is Mullins House, where someone with imagination in the early nineteenth century made a home around a disused mill wall. Since 1963, when Mullins was bought by Joseph L. Eastwick, Chairman of James Lees and Sons of Bridgeport, Pennsylvania, a magnificent country house has been erected, making full use of the old mill. Mullins is one of the happiest achievements of Robertson Ward Associates, the architects responsible for the restoration of Holders and the modernisation at Byde Mill, St Philip, where another old mill wall has been used as a changing room for the swimming pool. Mullins has its own beach house on Gibbs Beach. Arches, wooden balusters and welcome steps blend in happy harmony at Mullins reconciling old and new features of Barbadian architecture.

On the outskirts of Speightstown are several houses of special interest. Leamington is the residence of the United States ambassador, Bellerive the home of Claudette Colbert, and Hull House the home of Verna Hull. The beach house at Leamington, which is surrounded by some of the tallest coconut trees on the island, conforms to the Messel formula for indoor-outdoor living. Bellerive retains the Barbadian gallery, stone steps and circular drive common to many old style Barbadian houses but has been extensively altered. Hull House nestles close to it, completely renovated.

Speightstown, commonly pronounced Spikestown, was named after an early settler, whom the actor Robert Speaight on a visit claimed to be an ancestor of his family. Another appellation, 'Little Bristol', was used at a time when there was much trade between Bristol in England and the small Barbadian port. Nowadays it has been completely effaced by the familiar Spikes. Although Speightstown, like Bridgetown, has been altered latterly by the expansion of the island's economy, its streets still retain some of the atmosphere of earlier Barbados. Overhanging balconies have survived in wide streets with window bars, jalousies and supporting struts. Hawkers are less regimented than in Bridgetown and offer their fruit from open trays while they 'pass the time of day' conversing with their neighbours. Companionship not profit seems as much a motive of Barbadian hucksters today as it was one hundred years ago. In Speightstown only the motor car is ever in a hurry. The old pier, where droghers used to be loaded, survives and is used by fishermen. Another further along by Six Men's warehouse was used commercially until the fifties. No one has yet explained why the bay was called Six Men's, although some believe that six Indian men were found there by the first English settlers. It is also possible that the name derived from some sensational incident in Barbadian history which is no longer remembered. At least one other Barbadian place name has such an origin, Cut-Throat Village in St Thomas, which records the murder of Mr Elcock by his valet Godfrey whom he had manumitted in his will, but not during his lifetime.

Beaches continue along the coast beyond Six Men's, with occasional interruptions from coral outcrops. The most spectacular to be reached before Harrison Point, the island's most extreme westerly tip, is that of Maycock's Bay. This bay was heavily defended during the early years of English occupation but only a few crumbling stones of its fort have survived.

The frequency of open beaches on the northwest required frequent fortifications. Another fort was built at Chequer Hall Hill to guard Hangman's Bay while Half Moon Fort protected the beautiful sandy beach of Freyer's Well Bay.

Implements used by Arawaks during their period of settlement on Barbados are still discovered on the beach at Maycock's Bay.

Behind Friendly Hall, which is at the extreme end of Maycock's and Harrison Point, is an American Naval Facility. It looks down upon Mother's Day Bay. Activities at the Facility are little publicised, but the presence of American sailors since the 'fifties has given a great fillip to the economy of north-west Barbados. The letters which they write home in praise of Barbadian beaches and people persuade many a North American to choose Barbados when they have decided to take a Caribbean holiday.

Other West Coast American residents who have made their presence beneficial to Barbados are the Franciscan Sisters of the Sorrowful Mother, who run a school at Speightstown and an ultra-modern hospital dedicated to St Joseph in the grounds of a former plantation, Ashton Hall. It cost over three million dollars to build in 1964 and was designed for 135 patients. Of all who have befriended Barbados during this century few can have done more than these hard-working, hard-praying sisters from Milwaukee, Wisconsin.

8 The North and the Scotland District

St Lucy, the northern parish where Catholics were herded together in the early decades of settlement, and St Philip, the largest parish on the south-east coast, are lowlands interrupted periodically by hills and caves. Their cliffs receive the full shocks of immense rollers which beat upon them endlessly whenever the Atlantic Ocean is disturbed. Then white horses may be seen pounding in frantic gallops towards the land.

Cotton and aloes are crops most suited to the thin soils of these parishes and tobacco continues to be grown near the boundaries of St Lucy, in the Boscobel district of St Peter.

These desolate northern areas of Barbados were considered suitable by Puritan rulers as penal settlements for Irish Catholics whom Oliver Cromwell 'barbadosed' after he had grown weary of blood-letting in Ireland. He knew that the Puritans in Barbados would keep a close eye on them. The Minutes of Council for 1654-55 prove that a watch was kept. They record the arrival of three Irish priests landed at Spikes Bay to minister to Catholics in the north. Catholic priests were required by law to leave the island and the authorities who regarded the Irish as potential traitors in their midst probably hoped that the abundance of coves in the north might encourage them to attempt escapes by sea. It is certain that runaway slaves and servants from other parts of the island sought refuge in St Lucy because they knew they had more chance of getting away from Barbados if they could push off under cover of darkness from a secluded cove. They also took shelter in inland caves and copses.

Dr Alain Bombard chose one of St Lucy's coves, Stroud Bay, for his landing in the rubber dinghy *L'Hérétique*. He arrived the day before Christmas 1952 after a transatlantic crossing which he had undertaken in order to show the world that shipwrecked

24 and 25 *(opposite) Above: Altar and chancel of St Mary's, Bridgetown. Below: St Michael's Cathedral, Bridgetown*

sailors could survive at sea for much longer periods than was generally believed possible at the time.

Not far from Stroud Bay is Archers Bay. There a small group of inverted 'sugar loaf rocks' and a tiny coral stone island inhabited by sea-birds lend a touch of quiet beauty to a rustic pasture whose borders are unkempt agaves, a copse of whitewood trees, a small stony bay and giant casuarinas. Because of their great height casuarinas are known locally as mile trees. They were introduced into Barbados and other islands from Australia to act as windbreaks but soon became popular as ornamental plants. They are now grown everywhere, and may be seen as giant sentinels upon escarpments or as close-cropped dwarf hedges. Most frequently casuarinas are planted as border trees in avenues or as markers to denote property boundaries. Normally the wind soughs gently through their long pencil fronds but they react violently to high winds, bending and sweeping against the sky. In St Lucy and St Philip casuarinas offer refreshing shade and downy couches for those who have leisure to enjoy their friendly hospitality during picnics.

At the extreme northern point of Barbados two caverns have been bored through by pounding Atlantic rollers during centuries of high tides. They are collectively described by map makers as the Animal Flower Cave. In the lucid pools of these two caverns once thrived a 'garden' of 'sea anemones'. This pretty flower title is the common name of a marine worm which resembles a flower when its tiny tendrils are expanded. From a gerbera-like flower the seaworm becomes an inconspicuous rubber-like tube the moment a pointed finger draws near. Frequency of visitors with pointing fingers gradually discouraged the seaworms, who prefer now to inhabit remote sea gardens in less accessible parts of the coasts of Barbados.

The Animal Flower Cave is approached by stone steps on the land side. A gate above is normally kept locked because there is danger from high tides. Local guides will accompany visitors for a small fee to see the curious shaped stalactites and stalagmites and to admire the reflection of blue sky on the translucent pool in the far cavern. Above on the escarpment to the east of the cave a visitor can see several splendid gushes of white spume rushing skywards as the billows burst upon rocky ledges at the

26   and 27 (opposite) Scotland District. Above: Sugar cane near Canefield, St Thomas. Below: Looking towards Belleplaine on the East Coast

Spout near River Bay. Jets of water have been known to rise as high as 40 feet into the air.

Around Abbott's Bay, which lies half way between North Point and the Spout an olympic-size swimming pool, tennis court and restaurant are the main features of a resort complex which was originally designed for people who enjoy outdoor living in natural surroundings. Because of its remoteness from the main population centres and the absence of sandy beaches the land southwards from Chandler Bay to Green Pond by Morgan Lewis Beach is the least explored in Barbados. It is perhaps the most wild and the least unspoilt and is best seen from the sea.

Near the centre of this wild stretch of land is a diminutive peak called Pico Teneriffe. It rises like a large bump on a rugged eroded cliff. Anyone who has seen the towering mountain at Teneriffe in the Canary islands must wonder at the imagination of the person who first gave Pico Teneriffe its name. Yet, situated where it is on the south side of the deeply indented Gay's Cove, the peak seems higher than its few hundred feet while the figure on its pinnacle may be mistaken on a misty day for a sorrowful Madonna gazing out to sea in anxious care of her beloved fisher folk. The beach at Gay's Cove can be approached by a winding goat track. Few want to make the journey for the beach consists not of sand but of rounded stones which roar and shudder at every thrust and eddy of the tide. Not far inland from Gay's Cove is Mount Gay from which a famous Barbados rum gets its name.

A popular approach to Cherry Tree Hill from Speightstown is by way of Mile and a Quarter. The road goes past All Saints Church where Arnold, one of the first settlers, lies buried. A steep ascent at Diamond Corner heralds the approach to St Nicholas Abbey where a mahogany-bordered avenue leads up to a splendid vista of the Scotland District at Cherry Tree Hill. It is a well tried route beloved of taxi-drivers. The view from Cherry Tree Hill is the finest panorama of its kind in the West Indies, but it would be a pity to see only Cherry Tree Hill and miss the humble twisting road which goes by way of Diamond Corner behind St Nicholas Abbey to Boscobel. There a large red-roofed Anglican church dwarfed by towering cabbage palm trees bestrides a hill encircling an ancient stone mill. In this picturesque coral stone mill the postal authorities have fitted a bright red post box. A public house would give this remote Barbadian hill village the look of a Yorkshire village green.

Inside the church plaques further the illusion with reminders of a departed squirearchy. Boscobel mill and church provide a fine setting for an unusual colour picture. It will certainly be different from the conventional beach and palm souvenirs which most tourists take on the sheltered coasts.

The road to the left of the church leads down to Pie Corner after twisting and turning about a landscape which is charged with thought-provoking places such as The Baltic, Date Tree Hill, The Risk and the Graveyard. The origin of these titles and of the mysterious 'Pie' is not given in guidebooks, but the names probably derive from local indentification of familiar happenings. From Pie Corner a road to the right leads out to the field from which to see Cove Bay and Pico Teneriffe.

The view from Cherry Tree Hill shows the extent of golden brown sandy beach which runs unbroken through towards Bathsheba. The Atlantic Ocean is seen from the Hill as an almost continuous splash of white spume curling smoothly to the shore as it sends up a haze of spray. The sublime seascape is enhanced by a background of tall hills and cliffs which many have likened to alpine highlands and which the people of Barbados know as the hills of Scotland. Because of its outstanding beauty the borders of Cherry Tree Hill and the rise at the top are favourite picnic sites. Visits there are therefore more enjoyable on working days. Absolute quiet is recommended if you want to see monkeys at play in the trees which lie between St Nicholas Abbey and the foot of Cherry Tree Hill. Patience will always be rewarded, but there could be several hours of waiting. From time to time monkeys cross roads which run through wooded glades all over Barbados. On Sandy Lane golf course an enterprising monkey has added new handicaps to the game by running off with balls during play.

Most visitors can get close enough to the private house of St Nicholas Abbey to notice the Dutch architectural influence of its exterior. The house was built in the seventeenth century when the Dutch were the mentors of the English plantation owners. Surprise has sometimes been expressed at the provision of two fireplaces in a tropical house, but St Nicholas Abbey is by no means exceptional. Other houses in the Scotland district have fireplaces, even some of those built in this century.

The district of Scotland extends for approximately 22 square miles and covers about one-seventh of the land of Barbados. It contains the whole parish of St Andrew, and parts of St Peter, St Joseph and St John. The visitor with a high-powered car will find Scotland the most fascinating part of the island to explore, especially if the car is allowed to follow its nose and stops are frequent. The roads of Scotland were traced out by oxen, camels and assenigos centuries ago and although most have good surfaces, twists and turns, and rises and falls are frequent. The way to drive is to dawdle along below the official maximum island speed limit of 30 miles per hour. Slow as it may seem to habitual users of motorways 25 miles per hour is the ideal cruising speed in the only district of Barbados to be liberally supplied with hills, forest glades, gorges, ravines and streams. From the highest viewpoints, 1,000 feet above sea level in the neighbourhood of Mount Hillaby, St Vincent to the west may be seen on days of exceptional visibility. In the soft light of evening just before twilight the sombre dark greens, browns and greys of the Scotland hills take on a colouring of quiet beauty reminiscent of more temperate climes. It is not surprising that Scotland found favour with many planters. As late as 1807 Lieutenant Waller of the Royal Navy described the landscape he saw from a vantage point near Mount Hillaby. From the brink of a precipice he looked down into 'dark dells and capacious ravines crossing the valley in all directions, here we beheld hills of the most fantastic form, everywhere overshaded with wood, whilst the level ground at our feet afforded numberless samples of the industry and wealth of the planters. Their mansions were rendered conspicuous on every height, by the tall cabbage trees and windmills grouped around them.' Much of the wood and several mansions have disappeared since then, but in Turner Hall Forest and in the great houses at Farley Hill, Apes Hill, Spring Head, Farmers, Dunscombe, Canefield, and Castle Grant memories of the high days of planter hospitality in the highlands of Barbados linger on. Some of the planters' homes and factories in the Scotland hills were swallowed up when the earth moved during landslides. One of the most impressive occurred near Boscobel in 1901 when nearly 100 houses and estate buildings were destroyed as 400 acres of land slumped downwards to sea level. As recently as 1938, 100 houses in Rock Hall village had to be abandoned as 50 acres of hillside began to move.

The instability of the Scotland soils has a long history which can be traced to deforestation, cultivation of precipitous slopes and overgrazing of low pasture areas. These activities increased the frequency of soil slipping on escarpments, breakage of coral layers and loss of land. Over-exploitation of forest trees magnified the damage, and further problems were created when sand and silt blocked the streams after heavy flooding by storm water. Additional handicaps to cultivation are oil seepages over relatively large areas and the presence of salt on others. Oil seepages can be seen by the roadside near the entrance to Turner Hall Wood and oil layers compressed like honeycombs are visible in a rock near to Swan Factory at the foot of the hill below Turner Hall Plantation. Oil-impregnated mud is easily visible on the right of the Saddle Back on denuded hillsides above Cattlewash.

Oil is found on Barbados because the island once formed part of the oil-bearing mainland of America. Geologists teach that the sands and clays of the Scotland area were deposited by flood water at the delta of a river. After a violent volcanic eruption the geological strata were contorted and oil impregnated mud filled valleys and depressions caused by earlier upheavals of land from the sea bed. The land was then engulfed in the sea for millions of years before it rose again.

Before 1870 heavy tar oil was produced at Dan near Cattlewash Beach on the East Coast. From 1896 till 1910 a local company obtained 25,000 barrels of oil from the Turner Hall lands. The British Union Oil Company over two decades, beginning in 1920, produced nearly 127,000 barrels and in 1947 a gas well from Turner Hall lands produced the first natural gas to be distributed to consumers in some parts of the island. The woods at Turner Hall had for centuries been famous for a 'boiling spring', where gas could be ignited to produce a flame. A search for oil in large commercial quantities was begun by Gulf Oil in 1951. Wells were drilled to a depth of 14,000 feet, but the company closed its operations after a few years and leased its rights to another American company which continues to extract oil in limited quantities and has fed new supplies of natural gas into the government's pipelines.

Turner Hall Woods is a small forest covering 50 acres of land on a spur which runs north east from Mount Hillaby at heights between 600 and 800 feet above sea level. The forest is half a mile in length and nearly one quarter of a mile wide. It is one of the semi-evergreen forests which are found elsewhere in the Caribbean, notably in Trinidad, in St Vincent, Cannouan, Carriacou, St Lucia, Dominica, Martinique and Antigua. Rainfall at Turner Hall varies between 60 and 70 inches per year. Among the large trees to be seen in the forest are Cabbage Palms, Spanish Oak, Beef Wood, Fustic, Candle Wood, Silk Cotton, Sand Box and Fiddle Wood. Some trees reach heights of 120 feet. At least 32 species have been identified by botanists in the forest and there are more than 30 species of shrubs. Most of the trees and shrubs of Turner Hall Forest also grow in the less frequented gullies of St Joseph, St Thomas and St Peter.

A picturesque route leads to Farley Hill Park from Speights-town by way of the Whim and Orange Hill. At Prospect a path winds downwards through a glade to Farley Hill House and grounds. Large by Barbadian standards Farley Hill House has welcomed many distinguished visitors including Queen Elizabeth II. Farley Hill used to be the seat of Sir Graham Briggs, a Barbadian planter who supported Pope-Hennessy's attempt to form a West Indian confederation. The historian James Anthony Froude, who visited it in 1887, described Farley Hill then as a palace 'with which Aladdin might himself have been satisfied, its drawing-room filled with rare and curious things, selected with the finest taste, pictures, engravings, gems, antiquarian relics, books, maps and manuscripts'.

The glory that was Farley Hill had faded by the time that Robert Rossen approved it as Bellefontaine, the Fleury home in the 20th Century Fox film presentation of Alec Waugh's *Island In The Sun*. Then for two months of 1956 the crumbling old 'palace' experienced a transformation as 300 persons worked under the supervision of art director John de Cuir from Hollywood and his assistant Walter Simonds to convert it into a mansion suitable for a sugar baron. A complete new gallery and stairway was constructed to face the lawn. An open veranda was added in front of the main entrance, where a huge *porte cochère* with overhanging roof bordered an artificial lake. The waterworks of Barbados had to pump hundreds of thousands of gallons of water into this lake daily for weeks because its bottom was porous. Special paints were flown in from the United States and used to transform ordinary green leaves until they looked through the camera lenses like scarlet flamboyant flowers and magenta bougainvillaea blooms. One flamboyant tree was delicately cut into numbered pieces at Crystal Springs on the St James Coast, transported to Farley Hill and there stuck back carefully together as a single tree growing alongside the *porte cochère*. Lorry loads of tropical plants were taken to Farley Hill at the time and permanent coral stone gates for Bellefontaine were erected on the brow of the Newcastle avenue of Royal Palms above Foster Hall and Beachmount Hill. They are there to this day. Farley Hill Park is now a place of recreation supervised by a government-aided commission.

From the elevated walk where a summer house had been built during the days when planters ruled Barbados magnificent prospects of the Scotland hills can still be seen. Halfway down the hill beyond Cleland on the way to Greenland an old disused mill was used as background for the wallet-scene of the film. Halfway between Greenland and Cherry Tree Hill at Morgan Lewis an artificial ruin was added by the film makers to the old windmill which the Barbados National Trust has since restored as an example of the many hundreds which used to dot the countryside of the island until the early decades of the twentieth century.

Belleplaine, though a population centre, is not honoured with the title of town or village. It has schools, church, medical centre, post office, shops and other services which are normally found in a town, but most Barbadians think of it as the place where the East Coast road begins.

From Belleplaine, which was the terminal station of the Barbados Railway until 1937, the modern East Coast Road overlays the old railway track as far as Cattlewash where it rejoins the road which goes back towards Chalky Mount on the right, and across Joes River bridge towards Bathsheba on the left.

Several sites on both sides of the East Coast which Queen Elizabeth II opened in 1966 are popular picnic places. They are most frequently occupied on holidays and weekends. The sea on the East Coast is considered dangerous even by local residents during high tides and deserves constant respect from visitors. At all times it is inadvisable for a visitor to go beyond the barrier reefs or beyond the breaking surf. Currents are unpredictable on this coast line and in places quick-sands have been experienced.

A few potters still live on Chalky Mount the rugged range of hills which hang over the roadway 571 feet above sea level. From the clays which abound in the Scotland district these potters mould and bake ashtrays, miniature 'guglets' and 'coal pots' for sale to visitors. The best time to see Chalky Mount is between 5 and 6 in the late afternoon when the declining sun colours the Scotland hills with spectacular lights and when there is a slight nip in the air from the sea breezes. To be there or on any Scotland hill at moonrise is to see Nature pure and clean. Behind Chalky Mount on higher lands at Bissex Hill the East Coast is visible north and south. Before conversion as a youth recreation centre, Bissex was a police station, where large imported Canadian horses of the Royal Barbados Police Force were kept. These splendid horses may be seen in Bridgetown on ceremonial and sporting occasions.

Welchman Hall in St Thomas on the outskirts of the Scotland district is the most accessible of all Barbadian gullies and ravines. It is maintained by the Barbados National Trust which for more than ten years has been active in preserving places of historic importance and scenic beauty.

Canefield House nearby is a slightly larger edition of the Williams family home, Welchman Hall, which was destroyed by the hurricane of 1831. The entrance to Welchman Hall Gully is by way of an orange grove. Stone steps lead through a garden of frangipani, bougainvillaea, balisiers, begonias, plumbago and thumbergia to the original forest. On the right the Elephant Stalactite is easily recognisable at a cave whose floor has been smoothed by feet of men and monkeys down the ages. On the way to the nutmeg grove the visitor will see macaw palms with multicoloured seeds and black spined branches and the unique cohune palm whose fruit resembles a lemon. Notice will also be taken of one of the tallest breadfruit trees to be seen in the West Indies. Nutmegs and cloves were introduced into Welchman

Hall Gully during the nineteenth century. The nutmeg trees were brought over from Grenada and the clove trees from Zanzibar.

Beyond the nutmeg grove is a calabash tree. The fruit of the calabash when dried was often employed by Barbadians of earlier times as substitute cups or basins in kitchens and bathrooms. Nowadays the calabash is chiefly used, as the lower parts of the maracas or 'shak-shak', by West Indian musicians. Stone steps at the far end of the gully lead up to a platform which looks outward to the East Coast. There is a small car park below.

Not far from Welchman Hall Gully is Cole's Cave, the most celebrated cavern in Barbados. Inside the roof is sometimes concave and smooth, sometimes uneven and set with stalactites which reach down to stalagmites on the floor. About 300 feet from the entrance is the Fork, leading on one side to a stream which flows into a basin called 'the Bath'. Local tradition suggests a submarine outlet for the cave. Sir Robert Schomburgk, a distinguished research worker of the last century, accepted the oft-quoted tale of a duck travelling underground from the Bath to Fontabelle on the West Coast, as possible, but not likely. No further evidence has come to light to change his verdict.

The East Coast at Bathsheba between Lakes and Conset Bay is the favourite retreat of Barbadians on holiday and is liberally provided with holiday or 'bay' houses where families spend between two weeks and a month each year. In recent decades some beautiful retirement homes have been built there. Of these the most famous is Andromeda. It is surrounded by landscaped gardens of great beauty and variety. Visitors are invited to approach Andromeda gardens by the upper entrance below the famous Newcastle avenue of cabbage palms. One of the first trees to be seen is a 'bearded fig', the tree from which the 'bearded' island is believed by some to have got its name. The *ficus lentiginosa*, as it is known to botanists, is a member of the banyan family. Orchids and ferns are met further inside and at Easter time clusters of vermilion lilies, like those which Gauguin celebrated in paint during his residence on Martinique, nod gaily in the breeze. These gorgeous flowers please the eye but their bulbs are deadly. From them the early Indian inhabitants extracted the poison with which they tipped their arrows for hunting game and fish. Another tree, the annato, bears fruit from which the Indians made paint to decorate their faces and which today are still bought by manufacturers of lipsticks.

An avenue passes through a grove with 80 varieties of hibiscus and leads to a Hong Kong orchid tree which bears bright purple Cattleya-like flowers.

An archway comprised of blue and white petrea and sweet smelling stephanotis conducts to a private swimming pool, and a lily pond beyond which a thin cascade of water flows down through leafy glades to a major pool below. A path winds around beds of dracenas, torch gingers and the plant known as orange bird of paradise. Inside an orchid house on the left of the path may be seen dendrodiums, phalaeopsis, oncidiums, brasavolas and many more varieties. Beside the house of Andromeda there stands a splendid frangipani tree which bears sweet smelling cream-coloured flowers. Water-lilies in the pool below keep their blooms until eleven in the morning.

Clumps of palms and wild bananas attract the visitor towards a small gorge where the water tumbles down in a silvery water-fall as it journeys down to Beachmount and the sea. Further down sun-kissed coconut fronds in a medley of brown, dark green and yellow hues give latticed views of blue sky and empurpled sea. In the months of winter ixoras, purplish-red ginger lilies and traditional Christmas red poinsettias add vibrant colours in this miniature garden of Eden. Near the exit beyond the coconut glade a cluster of English weeping willows seem sad exiles among bright bougainvillaeas and the laughing crotons whose multi-coloured leaves frolic in the trade winds. Before 11 in the morning and between 4.30 and 6 p.m. in the afternoon Andromeda is at its best. Light clothes are always recommended and serviceable boots and shoes are essential after rains.

Those who love birds as well as gardens can see humming birds and banana quits flitting from tree to tree in pursuit of fruit, insects or pollen. But these birds are common all over Barbados wherever they are made to feel welcome visitors, in private gardens or in the many copses or woods which break up the dense fields of sugar cane, green vegetables and ground provisions.

9 'The Bottom Half of the Ham'

A clean cut of hamshaped Barbados along a line beginning at the deepwater harbour and ending at Hillcrest, Bathsheba separates the places described in the three preceding chapters from the rest of the island.

The Atlantic coastline continues from Tent Bay to follow inlets, coves, cliffs, sandy beaches and coral reefs right along to Kitridge Bay. Then a collection of sandy coves and beaches shaded by tall coconut trees break through the line of cliffs until they open wide by Sam Lord's Castle, Beachy Head, the Crane and Foul Bay. No one knows exactly why a beautiful sandy beach was given so ugly a name, but it has been so called from earliest times. From Andromeda gardens the Atlantic coastline can be kept in sight by following the road which leads to Foster Hall, Martin's Bay, Bath and Conset Bay. Or further exploration might be made of the Cornish-type Bathsheba shores and of the fishing centre at Tent Bay. On most days between 2 p.m. and 3 p.m. catches of fish are beached there, offloaded, weighed and sold with admirable dexterity and speed only a few feet away from the pounding surf. On the breeze-cooled veranda of the Atlantis Hotel close by a visitor, refreshed by ice-cold beverages, can obtain dozens of colourful souvenir pictures for stills or movies. Tent Bay Bathsheba is one of those places which can never be developed. Nature has designed it as a fisherman's beach and a fisherman's beach it will always be.

A fascinating exit from Bathsheba is by the road which runs north of Hillcrest. At High Rock after a sharp left turn the road goes steeply up to St Elizabeth's village. Occasional panoramic sweeps of the East Coast appear during a climb which must be taken in low gear. A sharp right turn where the gradient ends will lead back to the road, which goes past open fields in Joes River plantation towards Horse Hill. At the foot of Horse

Hill a little beyond St Joseph's Church the aptly named Bowling Alley on the left twists steeply upwards through lush vegetation to another field where the Cotton Tower commemorates the family name of a former Governor, Viscount Combermere. It is an old signal station and is maintained by the National Trust. Further along by Malvern a road on the left ends in a parking area above Hackleton's Cliff. A break in the cliff wall below permits pedestrians to walk down to Dacres Hill through the woods.

At Malvern the road runs southwards past Edey's village and Clifton Hall to St John's Church, which stands four-square to the winds on the furthest point of the high cliffs that run almost in an unbroken line to end abruptly overlooking St Joseph's Church. From the cliff walls and the garden cemetery of St John's Anglican Church the Atlantic 800 feet below seems like a pond of dark blue water ruffled by sprigs of white froth which blow across its surface. On the left the eye can pick out the pencil-pointed peak of Teneriffe and over by the sundial at the extreme end of the cemetery on the right the lighthouse of Ragged Point. Beyond the lighthouse The Chair gouged into the cliffs marks the point where the island sets its course southwards.

Near St John's Church on a plantation named Clifton Hall in memory of the Cornish home where he lived before coming to Barbados, Ferdinand Paleologus grew cotton and prospered. Ferdinand was the son of Theodore of Pesaro and Cornwall. Theodore was a descendant of the second brother of Constantine XI who ruled as Roman Christian Emperor in Constantinople until his murder by Turks on 29 May 1453.

Ferdinand, a tall man, was churchwarden of St John's and surveyor of highways. He died in the seventh decade of the seventeenth century and was buried in St John's Church in a lead coffin in the vault of Sir Peter Colleton. When the church was demolished by the great hurricane of 1831, the huge corpse of Ferdinand was discovered embedded in quicklime with head lying to the west in accordance with the practice of the Orthodox church. The coffin was not moved into the churchyard until 1836, the year before Queen Victoria ascended the British throne. Not until 1906 was the Portland tombstone erected to his memory in the churchyard. A local historian, Eustace Shilstone, later queried the date of Ferdinand's death, putting it six years earlier in 1670.

The first church of St John's was begun in 1667 and was intended to cost the vestry '110,000 pounds of sugar'. Sir Richard Westmacott sculpted the beautiful monument which commemorates Elizabeth Pinder inside. The pulpit of St John's is made of four local woods, ebony, locust, mahogany, manchineel, and two imported woods, oak and pine. The armorial bearings on the floor date back to the earliest church whose rector had been appointed in 1653.

Splendid views of Conset Bay are seen from Coach Hill, which leads down to a point where the road from Newcastle and Bath begins to climb upwards towards Sargeant Street and Codrington College.

The first Christopher Codrington went to Barbados from England and bought land in St John's in 1642. He made a large fortune and his elder son Christopher became deputy governor of the island in 1668 and later commander and governor of the Leeward Islands. A marble slab with the single word Codrington, and a famous library at All Souls, Oxford, commemorates his son, Christopher, who also became Governor of the Leeward Islands and who died in the mansion overlooking Conset Bay on Good Friday of the year 1710.

In his will Codrington had desired the Society for the Propagation of the Gospel in Foreign Parts to have his Barbadian plantations continued 'intire and 300 negroes at least always kept there, and a convenient number of Professors and scholars maintained there, all of them to be under vows of poverty and chastity and obedience, who shall be obliged to study and practice Physic and Chirurgery as well as Divinity, that by the apparent usefulness offered to all mankind they may both endear themselves to the people and have the better opportunities of doing good to men's souls, whilst they are taking care of their bodies'. Codrington's wishes have never been fulfilled at Codrington College, but a small educational institution financed from his estate developed into today's Lodge School, while a college opened in 1830 under supervision of Bishop Coleridge and was affiliated to Durham University in 1875. A number of doctors and Anglican priests have graduated from Codrington, but the finances of the college oscillated through the centuries with the ups and downs of sugar markets. Losses were also caused by hurricanes and other disasters. For a little more than a decade an order of Anglican monks attempted to convert Codrington College into a spiritual armoury of the Anglican Church but they left in the early 'seventies. There is an air of quiet and peace inside the chapel. Outside the lilies in the pool are gay and beautiful when in bloom. It is hard to recognise in the pasture on the other side the 'most sporting golf course' which was publicised in *The Times* of London in 1909 as a bait for English tourists.

The road behind the College is not always in good repair, but it drops directly down to the fishing centre and local resort at Conset Bay. There the blue Atlantic rolls ceaselessly in swathes of curling white foam towards the shore. On the right of the bay a path leads behind a private house through dense woods to a clearing of translucent pools and reefs bedecked with green and brown ribbons of seaweed.

Because of its location the church of St Mark's overlooking Conset Bay and College Savannah is worth visiting and an interesting though bumpy ride may afterwards be taken along cane tracks of Fortescue Plantation to Skeete's Bay, which is a picturesque fishing centre. On the other side of Skeete's Bay beyond the grounds of the old mansion of Whitehaven, Culpepper Island, a small coral rock, stands surrounded by sea within wading distance of the shore. Near Ragged Point Lighthouse the sea shudders inwards against the cliffs, waking echoes of sound as it does the other side of Skeete's Bay at Cummins Hole. The sea is impressive along this coast but the land is rocky and bleak, illuminated only when the bright flowers of the agave or Spanish needle are in bloom. The sourgrass which grows extensively around St Philip's eastern sea shore is beloved by 'grass-canaries', those yellow birds or warblers who are celebrated in a catchy calypso.

Until relatively recent times the castle which stands on the bluff between Long Bay and Dawlish was known as Long Bay Castle. Its thick walls had been constructed before the hurricane of 1831, which blew scaffolding for a distance of three miles to land on Three Houses Plantation. The builder, Samuel Hall Lord, was a pleasure-loving man who quickly spent the riches which he inherited through a chain of sudden deaths. He turned the small eighteenth-century plantation home of the Lords at Long Bay into an elaborate French-style mansion of the period. The traditional structure was approached by four flights of blue and white marble stairs and open porches. It took three and a half years to complete the plaster work of the ceilings inside. The work was done mainly by Charles Rutter and an assistant, Randalls. They received a little help from a militiaman, Warren.

The splendid ceilings of Sam Lord's Castle were at the time set off by fine pieces of Regency furniture, which were reflected in the large mirrors hanging on the walls in hand-carved frames. An old sales catalogue gives a glimpse of a banquet a century and a half ago. We can imagine old family portraits glimmering in the lights of candles flickering in high, delicately-wrought chandeliers. At the dining table 24 persons sit on Regency chairs and use silver cutlery to divide the meat heaped upon silver plates placed before them on a damask tablecloth laden with silver meat dishes. In the crystal glasses beside their plates red and white wine, poured from bottles stamped with the owner's name, sparkled in the candlelight and loosened tongues in a stream of anecdotes and gossip. Sam Lord created a park around his castle and introduced deer in the enclosure below the escarpment. A lithograph made from a drawing done by his niece Frances has preserved the deer park for posterity. In the lodges at the entrance to the castle Sam Lord kept carriage and horses. And on the beach close to the sea turtles swam in a crawl until they were summoned to the dinner table of the genial rake who owned them. Legend and fact intertwine about the person of Sam Lord whose name largely endures today because his castle was unique among the great houses of Barbados. In 1847 all that Sir Robert Schomburgk found to say of Long Bay Castle was that it was one of the finest mansions in the West Indies, its architecture of a peculiar style, its interior very tasteful and 'out of place in that part of the island, an oasis in the desert'. By then rumours that deaths of one nephew and two nieces had been unnatural no longer circulated in the island, while most people had forgotten the advertisement which appeared in a local newspaper of the year 1817 offering a reward for his capture to stand trial for 'perjury and forgery'. Sam was probably then living in England, where in 1808 he had married Lucy Wightwick in the Abbey Church, Bath. He was again living in England when he died on 5 November 1845 in Jermyn Street and his body was interred at Kensal Green cemetery.

There is no evidence that Sam Lord caused a single wreck on the Cobblers Reef, near Long Bay beach. Yet no less than 16 wrecks are known to have happened between the years 1820 and 1841. Always in search of income Sam Lord probably did encourage his servants and slaves to rescue for his own enrichment as much of the goods and valuables as they could recover from the sea before the officials in charge of wrecks arrived at Cobblers Reef. But there is no certainty even about this. The legends about Sam Lord have been recorded in *The Regency Rascal*, whose author, Lieutenant-Colonel Drury, is better known for *The Flag Lieutenant*. Perhaps he might more fittingly have perpetuated Sam as 'A Barbadian Buck'. For Samuel Hall Lord was nothing if not a great spender who believed in living far beyond his means when in Barbados as well as in England. When he died he left debts of £18,000, a sum of staggering proportions if converted into a modern inflated sterling equivalent. Sam Lord's death occurred 12 years after the exploitation of slave labour had ended in Barbados.

Not until the great villas were built on the West Coast after the Second World War was such opulence ever to be seen again on the island. The landowning families who survived Sam Lord went on living in great houses on the plantations, but they learnt to adapt themselves to new standards which were being set by Englishmen during the respectable reign of Queen Victoria.

Towards the end of the century landowning families in Barbados were taking their seaside holidays at the Crane, a hotel built on a cliff which juts out to sea so far that the platform at the far end of the lawn resembles the top deck of an ocean liner. Because of this enviable position so near to and yet high above the sea the Crane Hotel quickly earned a reputation as the sanatorium of the West Indies, and attracted travellers from all over the Caribbean and beyond. The sandy beach below is still much beloved by local residents. Most visitors, however, prefer less

28   *and* 29 *(opposite) Above: seventeenth century mansion of St Nicholas Abbey, St Peter. Below: Farley Hill House as it was in the early twentieth century*

30 (right) Broom-
field House, St
Lucy

31 (left) Alleyne-
dale Hall, St
Peter

vigorous surf and take their pleasure beside the large swimming pool which has been built alongside the hotel.

The Crane got its name from the lifting machine which was installed on the pier at the foot of the Crane House hill but which a century's waves have almost buried in sand.

Several days of sea sounding ruled out Chancery Lane as a reliable landing site for the nearly 700 tons of guns and hardware which were brought to Barbados by sea for the launching of missiles in 1962. Instead a sea passage was blasted through Cobblers Reef into Foul Bay and on 6 August the United States *Lieutenant-Colonel John U. D. Page*, began to discharge the strangest cargo ever to reach the island in the shape of two 16-inch naval guns which had been removed from ships after their use at sea had been prohibited. From Foul Bay to a site between Paragon and Seawell runway the heavy armaments were moved by specially-constructed railway to be ready for the Higher Altitude Research Project which McGill University was then supervising in association with scientists from North America. Research work is now supervised by the University of East Anglia. From that August day in 1962 a new era of scientific experiment aimed at better understanding of the Earth's atmosphere at high altitude began in Barbados. As part of the project nearly $1,000,000 of radar equipment was installed at Seawell airport. Never before had the government of Barbados been given such an opportunity to delete Foul from the map of Barbados and change the unpleasant title to the more suitable and heavenly attribute of Harp. Perhaps some future map makers will slip Harp Bay for Foul, and end the disgrace which has been associated for centuries with one of the island's loveliest beaches. The Long Bay, which lies between the bluff of Paragon and Inch Marlowe Point, is more commonly known today as Chancery Lane beach. The Indian settlers in Barbados loved this beach and in recent years the area has regained popularity with developers. The beachfront and lands are being landscaped for residential and resort homes. The Spanish Melia chain of hotels in 1972 announced their intention to build 300 new apartments at Chancery Lane.

Behind Chancery Lane an 18-hole golf gourse has been landscaped on high ground between Durant and Gibbons for a resort

I

complex designed with room for private homes, apartments and hotels.

The beach known as Little Bay or Silver Sands has also been developed for tourists in recent years and a hotel now offers poolside as well as beach facilities. Between Oistins Bay and Hastings Rocks will be found the majority of Barbadian hotels, apartments and guest houses, sandwiched between the homes of residents.

Oistins is rapidly becoming the third town of Barbados and only the pressure of seasonal tides prevents its seaside from being built over completely. Apartment hotels are situated on both sides of the road on the Maxwell Coast, where the small hotels and guest houses play hopscotch among private residential homes and apartments. The density of holiday houses, apartments and hotels continues right through past Dover Woods and St Lawrence Gap to Worthing, Rockley Beach and down to the Garrison.

Between St Lawrence Gap and Worthing post offices, shops, branches of banks and large food fairs serve local residents, hoteliers and visitors. Another smaller shopping and banking area between Hastings House and the Ocean View Hotel provides amenities which are mostly used by visitors.

Motorists can avoid the traffic of the coastal route into Bridge-town from Oistins by taking a sharp right turn after descending Thornbury Hill on the way in from Seawell airport. The church on the bluff overlooking Oistins Bay is remarkable for an empty tomb near the main entrance. The trouble at the Chase vault began on 9 August 1812. When it was opened for the interment of Colonel Thomas Chase, two leaden coffins inside were discovered by workmen to be in an unusual position, while the coffin of an infant, Mary Ann Chase, had been moved from one corner of the vault to another. Twice in 1816 and again in 1817 a state of confusion was found when the vault was opened for burial of other members of the family. The Governor of Barbados, Viscount Combermere, was present on 7 July 1819 when the coffins had been restored to order after the interment of Thomasin Clarke. He made impressions with his seal on the cement which masons had put on the outside of the entrance to the vault. On 20 April 1820 Viscount Combermere visited the vault. The cement was unbroken, his seal intact. The Governor then commanded the entrance to the vault to be broken and sent a man inside. The man discovered one huge leaden coffin standing up and resting against the middle of the stone door. He also noticed the infant's coffin lying at the far end of the vault where it had been thrown with so much force that it had damaged the wall of the vault. The publicity associated with this official discovery caused the family to remove the coffins and to bury their dead elsewhere. The vault remains unused to this day.

Speculation has never ceased about 'the great coffin mystery' in Barbados, yet similar occurrences in Wiltshire and in St Michael's Cathedral, where *lead* coffins have also been discovered in disorder from time to time, suggest that gas from decomposing bodies and not malevolent spirits was responsible for the violent separations and disarray of the sober arrangements which were made by undertakers. Records in this church also show that the Reverend Penniston Hastings, father of the famous Indian administrator Warren Hastings, served as rector there and was remarried there.

The little nipple of land which runs from Hastings Rocks to the Royal Barbados Yacht Club encloses an area where soldiers from Britain lived and frequently died during their periods of service in Barbados. Some of the shields of British regiments still hang on the coral stone walls of St Patrick's Cathedral in Bay Street. Among them are those of the Connaught Rangers, the Royal Irish Regiment, the Prince of Wales Leinster Regiment, the Yorks and Lancaster Regiment, the Duke of Wellington's West Riding Regiment, the East Yorkshire Regiment, the North Staffordshire Regiment, the Leicester Regiment, the Royal Scots, the Royal Scots Fusiliers, the Royal Berkshire Regiment, the King's Shropshire Light Infantry, the Royal Sussex Regiment, the Royal East Kent, and the Bedfordshire Regiment.

Barbados did not owe its centuries of British overlordship to accident or isolation from other islands. The men who drilled on the Savannah also manned the forts at Maycocks, Half Moon, Ruperts, Six Mens, Sunderlands, Haywoods, Orange, Coconut, Denmark, Margarets, Clarendon, Queens, Valiant, Royalist, Yacht, Hallets, Fontabelle, James, Willoughby, Line, Ormonds, Charles, Maxwell, Oistins, Hoopers and Kendalls. The restored Charles

Fort, part of which is now used by the management of the Hilton hotel at Needham's Point, helps us to understand what George Washington meant when in 1751 he called Barbados an 'intire fortification'. The presence of British troops in Barbados until the year 1902 contributed largely to the development of a sense of tranquillity and security which encouraged investment. It also reinforced links with the Mother Country and helped Barbadians to appreciate English sports like cricket, horse riding, polo, shooting and fishing, while soldiers provided captive audiences for theatrical, musical and similar happenings devised by persons who were anxious to improve cultural and social standards of life.

Captain Vunberry, who came with his regiment to St Anne's from Australia, is said to have been responsible for the introduction of the casuarina to Barbados.

When the British troops left Barbados in 1902 the Barbados Volunteer Force continued to occupy some of St Anne's Barracks until the Barbados Battalion was formed in 1942 and brought directly under the War Office. The Battalion was disbanded in 1947 when the Barbados Regiment was formed. The first Honorary Colonel of the Regiment was the Princess Royal, who presented the Queen's and Regimental Colours at a parade on the Garrison in 1953.

No one knows exactly where George Washington stayed in Barbados when he and his half-brother Lawrence visited in 1751, although a house in Bay Street opposite the Yacht Club has for years been called the George Washington House. In his diary of 7 November 1751 the future President of the United States, at the time a 19-year-old Major in the British North American Army, wrote: 'we pitched on the house of Captain Croftan, Commander of James Fort'. On the following day 'came Captain Croftan with his proposals, which tho extravagantly dear my brother was obliged to give £15 per month in his charge, exclusive of liquors and washing which we find'.

The house, wrote Washington, was about a mile from the Town, commanding the prospect of 'Carlyle' Bay and all the shipping. It was also extensive by land. Before he contracted smallpox Washington was made a member of the Beefstake and Tripe Club, which in a revived form used to meet yearly during the 'sixties and will probably go on meeting in the future as a special link between Barbados and the first American President, who praised its beautiful prospects by sea and land.

The fort at Needham's Point which George Washington visited is now the site of the Barbados Hilton hotel. The Hilton has its own landing pier facing Bridgetown across the water from the old Engineers Pier which has been incorporated into the new Holiday Inn. This hotel, the largest near the city of Bridgetown, is managed by Commonwealth Holiday Inns of Canada. Being close to Brigetown the Hilton and Holiday Inn Hotels are popular with local residents whose social life and activities often merge with those of visitors. The two major yacht clubs in Barbados have headquarters on either side of the Holiday Inn. During the winter months the anchorage of Carlisle Bay attracts many dozens of trans-Atlantic yachts. Then crews quickly make friends among the local yachtsmen whose small vessels ride buoyantly for most of the year in Carlisle Bay. Nowhere perhaps is friendship more freely given by Barbadians today than by those islanders who spend many hours of their lives afloat on the blue waters which surround the sheltered coasts of Barbados.

The parishes of St George and St John together with St Michael, were from earliest times the most favoured by the squirearchy who directed the affairs of Barbados as Members of Parliament, judges and soldiers. They put their deep roots down in St George's valley more than 300 years ago, few owning less than 200 acres of the rich black soil which stretches along the six-mile area which runs between St George's church and St Philip's church. In this valley lived, among many others whose names are recorded in the well tended parish church of St George's, Grace Silvester, Sir Martin Bently, Rowland Bulkely and Lady Ann Willoughby.

Farther along on the 'topp of the cliff' as the raised plateau of St John was known lived other planters like Christopher Codrington, Henry Walrond, Henry Drax and Sir Peter Colleton. They belonged to the élite class of about 170 big planters who had by the year 1680 divided up the fertile lands of Barbados into patterns they still bear. They stood at the apex of an English society firmly based on class, whose lower pillars were some 200 medium landowners, 400 city dwellers, 1000 small planters,

1200 freemen, 2300 servants and approximately 40,000 slaves. The English landscapes of St George and St John, where even the sugar cane grass seems to be regimented and the eddoes stand in rows like Grenadier Guards on parade, will be their permanent memorial so long as agriculture continues to be the backbone of Barbadian life.

For whatever their shortcomings, these English squires loved the land and were not too proud to do penance before God when it did not yield abundant crops; as they did in the year 1663 when an act of theirs was proclaimed 'appointing a day of humiliation for imploring the seasonable blessings of God, under the present calamity of a long continuous drought.'

10 Barbados: General Information

Climate: Generally healthy: tropical, cooled by steady trade winds. Cool dry season from December to April, with occasional light showers. May and June are slightly warmer months but generally agreeable. July, August and September are the hottest and most humid months of the year and the periods of heavy rain and occasional storms. October and November are variable like May and June.

Rainfall averages 60 inches per year.

Day time temperatures average between 24°C (75°F) and 26.7°C (80°F), depending on the month, with night time drops between ten and fifteen degrees. Winds are generally cool at nightfall on east and south-east during winter months.

Population: 0.24 million. Population density over 1330 per square mile.

Government: Parliamentary democracy based on the United Kingdom pattern with a Governor General representing the Queen of Barbados. A House of Assembly of 24 persons is elected for single constituencies by adults who have reached the age of 18. A Senate of 21 is nominated, for the most part on the advice of the Prime Minister, for some part by the Leader of the Opposition, and to a lesser extent by the Governor-General.

Local government under the control of the central government. Barbados became independent on 30 November 1966 and is a member of the Commonwealth and of the Organisation of American States.

Education: Barbados has a literacy rate of 97%. About 86% of pupils are educated free of charge at primary or secondary schools which are owned or run by the State. The remainder are educated in government-approved private schools, which charge fees. Other educational facilities are provided at a Community College, a Polytechnic, extra-mural centres and the Cave Hill Campus of the University of the West Indies. There are special schools for the deaf, mentally retarded, and children referred by the Juvenile Courts.

Agriculture: Sugar cane, cotton and coconuts are the highest yielding export crops.

Corn is also grown in large quantities for consumption by human beings and animals locally. Other vegetables and root crops grown for local consumption are beans, peas, beet, cabbage, carrots, cucumber, lettuce, egg-plants (aubergines), squash, peppers, pumpkins, sweet potatoes, okras, yams, tomatoes, eschalots, onions and spinach.

Animal Husbandry: A modern pasteurised plant and feeding of pangola grass has increased the local supply of fresh milk.

Over 3,000,000 pounds of pork are produced annually and island poulterers satisfy almost the entire yearly demand for chicken meat and eggs.

Beef, veal and mutton are also produced locally.

Fishing: Flying fish, dolphin, snapper, king fish, tuna and other species are caught at different times of the year off Barbadian coasts in reasonable quantities. Other seasonal sea foods include turtle, lobsters, sea eggs, sprats and frays. Shrimps are exported to the United States by a locally owned company which distributes some of their catches in Barbados.

Industry: The production of sugar benefits more than 17,000 small sugar cane growers who cultivate 10,000 acres. Another 50,000 acres of sugar cane lands are divided up among approximately 200 plantations. A company with authorised capital of $50,000,000 (Barbadian), the Barbados Sugar Factories Limited, is responsible for the organisation and operation of 13 factories, two of which produce fancy molasses (syrup) and the remainder dark crystal sugar.

In crop time which varies between January and June the sugar industry directly employs over 15,000 persons. For the rest of the year 10,000 are retained. The bulk of Barbados sugar is sold to the United Kingdom. Less than 15,000 tons a year are consumed locally and on neighbouring islands.

Canada and the United States have bought more than 2,000,000 gallons of fancy molasses (syrup) from Barbados yearly over a five-year period and in 1970 more than 8,000,000 gallons of vacuum pan molasses were exported to North America. Vacuum pan molasses are also used locally to produce alcohol and rum. Barbados exports over half a million wine gallons of rum yearly. In 1966 exports exceeded one million gallons.

Tourism in 1970 employed 12,000 persons in a working population of 85,000 and approximately $400,000,000 Barbados dollars are now invested in tourist plant and equipment. In 1972 the island offered around 8,000 beds in a variety of accommodations.

In 1971 tourist earnings were £16,100,000.

Light Industries: A wide range of articles are manufactured locally, including beer, tobacco, soft drinks, biscuits, bread, ice-creams, textiles and furniture. More than 150 light manufacturing companies operate on government industrial parks and estates.

Barbados is a member of the Caribbean Common Market which in May 1973 comprised 12 Commonwealth Caribbean countries.

Electricity: is available to more than 90% of the population. Supply voltage is generally 115/200 but 115/230 volts is available in some areas. The electricity network extends over 750 miles. In 1971 sales were 145,000,000 KW hours. Over the five years beginning 1973 the Light and Power Company propose to increase general capacity by 80,000 KW at a cost of $50,000,000 (Barbados).

Natural Gas: The government-owned Natural Gas Corporation supplies over 5,000 consumers over a network of 88 miles. Imported propane gas in cylinders is available for other consumers.

Oil: Mobil Oil Barbados Limited manufactures gasoline, kerosene, diesels, fuel oil and asphalts for internal needs.

Telephones: Approximately 40,000 subscribing stations had been connected in 1972 by the Barbados Telephone Company Limited, a subsidiary of the Continental Telephone Corporation of the United States. Calls can be made to all countries with telephone networks.

Telecommunications: Cable and Wireless Limited operates international telecommunications to and from Barbados and collaborates with the Barbados Telephone Company in operation of telephone and telex services. The company has constructed a satellite Earth Station at Bath and has a main office complex at Wildey which has been designed to include an international switching centre for telephone calls and a message switching computer for telegraph traffic. Through a communication satellite in stationary orbit 22,300 miles over the Atlantic, Barbados has direct links with Jamaica, the United Kingdom, the United States and Canada. The Earth Station can carry more than 10,000 telephone channels, and can handle intercontinental colour and monochrome television.

Broadcasting: The government-owned Caribbean Broadcasting Corporation broadcasts 18½ hours daily on Radio Barbados and seven hours daily in full colour on CBC-TV. Barbados Rediffusion Service Limited, a subsidiary of Rediffusion Ltd., of London, operates a daily wire service.

The Press: The daily newspaper is owned by Thomson interests in Canada.

A monthly general interest magazine, *The Bajan*, and a half yearly literary magazine *BIM*, are also published. The Barbados Museum and Historical Society and the Barbados Chamber of Commerce publish journals.

Holidays and Festivals: New Year's Day, Good Friday, Easter Monday, Labour Day 1 May, Whit Monday, First Monday in August, First Monday in October, Independence Day (30 November), Christmas, Boxing Day (26 December). Additional holidays and half holidays for special occasions.

Language: Written English as modified by local custom. Spoken English, variable from precise academic style through a multiplicity of accents, Americanisms and Caribbean usage to vigorous 'Bajan' dialect.

Local Courtesies and Customs: Each Barbadian counts. The friendliness a person displays is directly proportionate to the warmth of address he receives. The Barbadian reflects before he speaks.

It helps to say 'good morning' first and to ask permission before taking photographs. You are also requested to wear reasonable dress when in the city centre, business houses, churches, or anywhere where local customs prevail.

Medical Facilities: As good as many places and sometimes better than most.

Water: Adequate and safe. Fresh from taps. No mineral flavour.

Laundry and Dry Cleaning: Adequate and prompt.

Tipping: Always welcome. Service charge normally added in hotels and restaurants.

Transport: Barbados has over 600 miles of roads which are kept in a fair state of repair.

Scooters, bikes, mokes and cars are available for hire.

Driver's licences have to be checked with police and a permit obtained. It is advisable to hire only vehicles which carry full comprehensive insurance, and to agree prices in advance.

For ordinary journeys use taxis with meters.

The local buses are relatively cheap, but are crowded during peak hours.

Always drive on the left and blow your horn in country districts as a greeting. Speed limit 30 mph over most of the island, reducing to 20 mph and 10 mph in city areas. One-way traffic operates in Bridgetown.

Service Clubs and Organisations: Rotary, Lions, Canadian Women, American Women, Soroptomist, Alliance Française, Hispano-Alliance, Junior Chamber of Commerce, Jaycettes, British Red Cross, YMCA, YWCA, RSPCA, Youth Town, Council of Women, Toastmistresses, Business and Professional Women's Club, National Trust, Pharmaceutical Society, Law Society, Bar Association, Automobile Association, Victoria League, Arts Council, Horticultural Society, US Navy Wives, Royal Commonwealth Society.

Sports Clubs and Associations: Amateur Athletic, Olympic, Lawn Tennis, Cricket, Amateur Football, Netball, Basketball, Boxing Board of Control, Amateur Weightlifting and Body Building, Cycle Union, Turf Club, Show Jumping Federation, Hockey Association, Motor Cycle Association, Polo Association, Rugby Club, Sailing and Cruising Club, Yacht Club, Rockley Golf Club, Sandy Lane Golf Club, Light Aeroplane Club, Swimming and Water Polo, Small Bore Rifle Club, Rifle Association, Rally Club, Game Fishing, Water Ski, Darts League, Table Tennis, Bridge, Mayfair Bridge Club, Kennel Club.

Documents Required: All visitors (except from the United States) need a valid international certificate of vaccination. Immigration officials request passports from all visitors except citizens of the United Kingdom, United States and Canada who stay for periods under six months and possess a return ticket (UK visitors require passports for re-entry to their own country).

West Indian police permits are accepted from West Indian citizens.

Getting to Barbados: BOAC and ICA from UK and the mainland of Europe; Air Canada and WARDAIR from Canada; BWIA, Eastern Airlines and Pan American from the United States; provide scheduled air services for long-distance travellers.

Connecting services are also provided by Air France, KLM, VIASA, SAS, CARIBAIR and LIAT.

Charter flights are frequent.

Barbados is popular with cruise passenger ships. Limited sea travel is available to Europe, North America and other countries.

Currency: The Barbados dollar. At time of writing $4.80 was equivalent to £1 sterling.

Religion: Many Christian denominations, Jew, Moslem and Hindu.

Time: Five hours behind GMT from April to September, otherwise four. One hour ahead of Eastern Standard Time.

USEFUL TIPS

In flight: Do not take alcohol and tranquillisers together. Fill in landing card before arrival.

Stock up with duty free goods sold in flight.

On arrival: Walk slowly to terminal buildings.

Be patient and good tempered with health, immigration and customs authorities (if you have anything to declare).

Leaving airport: Check whether taxi has meter and that tariffs are displayed prominently. If not fix price in advance (inclusive of bags) in Barbados dollars. Use Barbados dollars for payment always. Money can be changed at the airport.

Health advice: Eat and drink modestly on first day. Treat the sun with respect, especially between noon and 3 p.m. Use anti-sun lotion and wear polaroid sun shades. At sea wear floppy hat to protect back of neck and keep a towel handy to drape around shoulders.

Warnings: Deposit valuables in hotel safe. Do not leave them around indoors or outdoors.

Never go beyond your depth in sea with strong currents.

Wear soft shoes when walking over coral reefs.

Remember sea moss is slippery.

Avoid contact with sea eggs, black or white, and shun Portuguese men-of-war when bathing.

Do not eat strange fruit or berries, especially manchineel fruit: do not lie on 'dead' sand.

Money: Exchange money at banks.

Shopping: Avoid visits to town on cruise-ship days. The best time to shop in the city is early morning or after lunch Mondays to Thursdays. Thursday is early closing day for some stores.

Photographers: Use hood always on camera and ultra-violet or other filters on lenses. Try polaroid lens for sea-water shots. Keep film in air-conditioned rooms. Never leave camera in trunk of car, unless it is parked under shade.

Leaving: Check travel documents; weigh travelbags, buy duty-free goods. Keep sales slips and put all dutiable items in one bag. Goods purchased in Bridgetown have to be collected at airport, so shop one day before departure.

Road Manners: Remember pedestrians use the roads to walk in and may resent motorists who 'can't wait!' Check parking areas in city. Use high-powered cars in the highlands.

Dress: Light clothes are worn throughout the year. Light mackintosh or umbrella during rainy season. Two swimsuits are useful, one for morning, one for afternoon.

SPECIALLY RECOMMENDED

Places to eat:

Lunch: *Ocean View*; intimate, on sea. Excellent local food.
         Hilton; self service, tourist atmosphere.
         Dolly's, Landsend; good food and service.
         N. E. Wilson's Roof, Bridgetown; snacks.

Dinner: *La Bonne Auberge*, St Philip.
         Bagatelle Great House, St Thomas.
         Sandy Lane, St James.
         Greensleeves, St Peter.
         Pisces, St Lawrence.
         Ascanio's, Rockley.

For best service, book table in advance, order wine. To avoid embarrassment check prices, wine list, tipping, etc. before arrival. Value for money is never cheap.

Sea Excursions: Jolly Roger Cruises from Careenage up West Coast 11 a.m. to 4 p.m. Book day before. Sunset cruises also offered.

Tennis Courts: Sandy Lane, Hilton, Paradise Beach, Sunset Crest, Garrison.

Golf Courses: Sandy Lane, Rockley, Barbados Golf and Country Club, Gibbons.

Horse Riding: Chandler Riding Stables, Brighton.
Mrs Clarke, Moonshine Hall, St George.
Mrs Angela Williams, Mangrove, St Philip.

Sea Sports: Carlo Water Sports, Hilton.
Willie Hassell, Paradise Beach.
Sandy Lane Hotel.

Deep-Sea Fishing: Telephone 73913 (Fisherman's Corner) to charter *The Gunner* or telephone 21274 to charter the *Emma Maureen*.

Evening Entertainment:
Barbecue and Floor Show, Miramar, Paradise Beach, Caribbean Pepperpot, Sandy Lane, Hilton, Holiday Inn. Check times in free hotel newspaper.

Cruise Passenger Beaches: Hilton, Paradise Beach.

The Arts: A group of dancers, 'The Sun Movement', Folksingers, Choral Society, Art Exhibitions, Police Band, Barbados Museum, Bridgetown Library, Amateur Theatre.

Planetarium: Harry Bayley Observatory, Clapham.

Shopping, Bridgetown: Harrisons, Da Costa, Cave Shepherd, Stechers, West Indies Handicrafts, Louis L. Bayley, Mount Gay.

Drive Yourself Excursions:

From South Coast: *Tour One*
Rendezvous Hill—Kent House—St David's Church—Staplegrove
—Frere   Pilgrim—Boarded   Hall—Bulkeley—ST   GEORGE'S
CHURCH—Gun Hill—Cottage—Ashbury—Four Cross Roads—
Verdun (Presentation College)—ST JOHN'S CHURCH—Coach Hill
—Sargeant Street—Codrington College—Thicket—Three Houses
—Sandford—Trinity Church—SAM LORD'S CASTLE—THE
CRANE—Rices—Kirton—Four Square—Highway 6—Bannatyne
—Aberdare—Lyrias—Rendezvous Hill.

From South Coast: *Tour Two*
Top Rock—Maxwell Hill—Kendall Hill—Wotton House—Banna-
tyne—Lower Greys—Brighton—French's—Byde Mill—Stewart
Hill—Society—Colleton—ST JOHN'S CHURCH—Newcastle—St
Margaret's Chapel—Foster Hall—ANDROMEDA—St Elizabeth's
—Joe's River—Horse Hill—Blackman's—Andrews—Groves—
Cottage—Gun Hill—St George's—Constant—Stepney—Egerton
St Davids—Bannatyne—Kingsland—Silver Hill—Gall Hill—
OISTINS—Top Rock.

From Bridgetown
Codrington Hill—Warrens—Jackson—Sharon Chapel—Rugby—
Hopewell—Holy Innocents' Church—WELCHMAN HALL—
Sturges—Bloomsbury—The Saddle Back—CHALKY MOUNT—
Belleplaine—St Andrew's Church—Swann Factory—Turners
Hall—Farmers—Porey Spring—Dukes—Shop Hill—SHARON
CHAPEL—Canewood—Hothersal Turning—Waterford.

From the West Coast: *Tour One*
Holetown—Trent—Orange Hill—Gregg Farm—White Hill—
Mount All—Baxter—Bruce Vale—Belleplaine—EAST COAST
ROAD—Cattlewash—Spring Field—Parks—The Saddle Back—
Bloomsbury—Carrington—Canefield—Lion Castle—Rock Hall—
St Thomas's Church—Lascelles—Holetown.

From the West Coast: *Tour Two*
Gibbs Beach—Eastry House—Bakers—Sailor's Gully—The Rock—
Four Hills—Indian Ground—Prospect—Farley Hill—Greenland—
Morgan Lewis—CHERRY TREE HILL—Portland—ALL SAINTS
CHURCH—VILLA MARIA—Speightstown.

32 *East Coast, Barbados seen from a point near Beachmount Hill*

33 (right) The Old Military Prison near Garrison Savannah is now the headquarters of the Barbados Museum

34 (left) Completed in 1947, British architect Geoffrey Jellicoe designed this Palladian palace facing Heron Beach

From the West Coast: Tour Three
Speightstown—The Whim—Whitehall—Mount Brevitor—Prospect—Farley Hill—Portland—Diamond Corner—Boscobel—The Graveyard—Pie Corner—GAYS COVE—Pie Corner—Spring Hall —St Lucy's Church—Alleyndale—Rose Hill—Jerusalem—Maynards—SIX MEN'S BAY.

PLACES OF SPECIAL INTEREST:

North of a line Speightstown to Long Pond:
Hospital: St Joseph's Hospital, Villa Maria.
Colleton House: Stables.
Bromefield House: near Maycock's Bay. Old Barbadian great house.
Harrison Point Lighthouse: Most western part of Barbados.
Stroud Bay: Landing place of Dr Alain Bombard.
Archer's Bay, Animal Flower Bay, The Spout, Pico Teneriffe: places of natural beauty.
Boscobel Church. Morgan Lewis Mill: Places of historic value and scenic attractions.
Cherry Tree Hill: window on the Scotland district and East Coast.
Farley Hill: government park, with panoramic view of Scotland hills.
Coleridge and Parry School: Boys' secondary school.
Alleyndale Hall, St Nicholas Abbey: old Barbadian mansions.
All Saints Church, Villa Maria Church, St Peter's Church: old and modern places of worship.

North of a line Paynes Bay to Ragged Point:
Mount Misery, Mount Hillaby, Castle Grant, Hackletons Cliff: highlands over 1,000 feet.
Satellite Earth Station: near Bath.
Turner Hall Woods, Foster Hall Woods: forests.
East Coast Road: Between Belleplaine and Cattlewash.
Luxury hotels: West Coast.
Luxury homes: West Coast.
Chalky Mount: potteries.
St James Church, St John's Church: old parish churches with fine memorials and historic interest.

K

Ragged Point, Culpepper Island, Skeete's Bay, Cummins Hole, Conset Bay, Tent Bay : places of scenic beauty, some used by fishermen.

Codrington College, Codrington (Girls) High School, Presentation (Boys) College, Lodge (Boys) Secondary School, Alexandra (Girls) Secondary School : educational institutions.

Holders : Polo Ground and Show Jumping Field.

Welchman Hall Gulley : botanic gardens and caves maintained by Barbados National Trust.

South of a Line Paynes Bay to Ragged Point :

Cave Hill University Complex : Law Faculty and Colleges of the University of the West Indies and Centre for Multi-Racial Studies of the University of Sussex.

Secondary Schools : Harrison's (Boys) College; Queen's (Girls) College, Combermere (Boys) School, St Michael's (Girls) School, St Ursula's (Girls) School, St Winifred's (Girls) School, St. Gabriel's (Girls) School.

Teachers Training College : Erdiston College.

Samuel Jackman Prescod Polytechnic.

Sports Grounds : Kensington Oval, Fontbelle; Stadium, Waterford; Racetrack, Savannah.

Historic houses : Warrens, Drax Hall (old staircase).

Parks : Queens, King George V, Farley Hill.

Churches : St Michael's Cathedral (sculpture and inscriptions); St Patrick's Cathedral (statue from St Pierre, Martinique); St George's Church (painting by Benjamin West).

Military fortifications : St Anne's Barracks, Military Cemetery, Gun Hill, Fort St George, Fort Charles.

Barbados Museum : Old Military Prison.

Harbour : Fontabelle.

Airport : Seawell.

Government Buildings : concentrated between Fontabelle and Hastings.

Hospitals : 600 bed Queen Elizabeth Hospital; 135 bed St Joseph Hospital.

Industrial Parks : Grazettes (12 acres), Newton (22 acres) Harbour Industrial Park (26 acres), Seawell Industrial Park (20 acres), Pelican Industrial Park for cottage type industries (near Harbour).

III POSTSCRIPT

11 People, Language, Fauna and Flora

A pride that makes no wanton boast
Of what it has withstood;
That binds our hearts from coast to coast:
The pride of nationhood.

These words of the anthem are intended to encourage pride in the 'blessed rock' which is cherished the more because of the sufferings and endurance of Barbadian forefathers. From pride stems that optimism which is the official creed of the islanders, who may also draw confidence from the belief that the Lord is 'on the people's side'. Optimism is also natural for a people who are never more than seven miles away from the blue Caribbean sea and whose waking hours are spent in the sunshine of perpetual summer.

Yet the pressure of people on a small land area, more than 1330 per square mile, prevents the Barbadian sinking down to the level of a native of Lotusland. He cannot rely on a mango dropping into his mouth as he sits relaxing under a tree. Barbadians must accept the need to work for a living and whenever incentives are great enough may even work harder than most. The basic philosophy of the Barbadian, however, is that enough is as good as a feast and that when there is a choice between work for work's sake and work to satisfy human needs it is better to choose the latter alternative.

This innate Barbadian philosophy, which may have arisen from a long history of forced labour and servitude, helps to explain the Barbadian fondness for laughter and freedom and to eat, drink and be merry at all times. The standpipe laugh, a deep-throated explosion of air sucked from the belly which explodes in great guffaws, is symptomatic of a zest for life which is peculiarly Barbadian. The refinements of Barbadian élites and bureaucrats have

nothing in common with this fundamental mood of the Barbadian proletariat whose recent enfranchisement at the early
age of 18 is bound to alter traditional bourgeois political and
social concepts. The evolution of a new Barbadian society is still
in its infancy and it is unlikely that the impact of persons born
after independence will be felt until the middle 'eighties.

By then much that is still old Barbados will have been transformed by changing patterns of education, the creation of
new social pyramids and the influences of new world moods.
Meanwhile it is relevant to comment on the survival of Barbadian
word forms which derive from the experience of generations of
workers on the land. Older Barbadians who never attended the
neat modern schools of today still use double-nouns to emphasise their meanings. They talk of 'rock-stones' for stones, or
'ram-goats' for rams, of 'bull-cows' for cows, of 'fowl-cocks' for
cocks, and of 'cock-a-roach' for roach. This directness of speech
forms is allied to the description of Barbadian flora. Barbadians
in all walks of life know what plants and trees carry the names
of woman's tongue, wonder of the world, soap-berry, bread and
cheese, cannonball, bellyache bush, forbidden fruit, cure for all,
duppy bush, clammy cherry, fat pork, hug me close, stinking
missy and, of course, the mile tree.

Vividness of description applies not only to the trees and
flowers, but is also a quality of all Barbadian speech. There is
a torrent of welcome in the friendly greeting of a neighbour
who says 'glad to hear yuh mout' when she meets a friend who
has been sick. There is an impetuous overflow of disapproval
when a talkative acquaintance is told 'yuh mout running like a
burst pipe'. From the rich treasury of such primitive speech
forms Barbadian authors like George Lamming and Austin Clarke
have carved vital memorials of a people whose capacity for
survival is partly explained by their capacity to be triumphantly
human and vocal.

It is the broad humanity of the Barbadian, his freedom from
the artificialities of the bourgeois life, that generated the legend
of his being the friendliest of Caribbean people.

Some recognition may also be given to the common sense of
the peasants from Europe who throughout centuries modified
their own culture patterns to establish bridges of tolerance

whereby a policy of 'live and let live' could strengthen until in churches, chapels, and schools and everywhere on playing fields, differences of race were obliterated in pursuit of nobler ideals. But for the survival of relatively large numbers of white poor on the island of Barbados the clash of economic disparity between have and have-not might have produced those dreaded blood-baths which were constantly feared in the age of slavery. To-gether white poor, black poor, and an infinite variety of coloured poor toiled, sweated and dreamed dreams of a society where they might have a larger slice of the national cake. If today some of their descendants find themselves in seats of power and affluence they owe it chiefly to those of their forefathers who overcame the many obstacles placed by vested interests, who naturally resented such challenges to their privileged state.

It is less easy to explain how so small an island as Barbados has produced so great a number of cricketers of international repute, and in Garfield Sobers and Sir Frank Worrell two of the greatest of all times. Compared to their achievements in cricket, the production of an Editor of *The Times*, a permanent Under Secretary of State to administer home affairs in Britain, hundreds of West African civil servants, a United States Congressman and some authors and poets, seem small matters. Perhaps Sir Grantley Adams, a Barbadian who won international recogni-tion for his political achievements, spoke words of truth when he said that 'cricket is the religion of Barbados'. For undoubtedly the cricketer who is circumscribed by rules approved by gentle-men is bound by standards of conduct which equate to 'playing the game'. The quality of Barbadian life and its codes of conduct owe as much to cricket as to any other single activity. The game of life follows the rules of cricket.

For those who have neither time nor inclination to probe so deeply into the Barbadian character other attractions beckon among its flora and fauna. The island of Barbados is populated by other living creatures besides men and women. There are do-mestic animals and pets in many homes besides multitudes of dogs and cats, hundreds of horses, mules and donkeys and thousands of cows, sheep and goats. These animals, like hens and chickens, are dependent on man. Other wild animals look after themselves and reap what they do not sow. Among them are monkeys, hares, mongoose, field rats and a small number of racoons.

Two enemies of garden lovers are the slimy slugs and wriggling caterpillars. Constant battles are waged against them. Gardeners instead welcome the cheerful lizards, friendly frogs and rare ladybirds. Leading choristers of night in gardens and open pastures are the whistling frogs and the crickets whose high-pitched notes rise above the lower hums of other insects who praise the gods of darkness.

By day the loudest noisemakers among winged creatures are flocks of grackles or blackbirds. Unlovely to look at, awkward in their gait, the blackbirds chatter, squawk and pounce their way across the island in endless search of food. The prettiest thing about them is their speckled green eggs!

By contrast the wood (or Zenaida) dove is a bird of peace, except when aroused in combat with another dove. Mostly the refrain of its low-keyed coo sounds like a chant of praise, so much so that Barbadians maintain that his message is that 'Moses spake God's word'. Less common than the wood dove is the quiet small turtle dove.

Most beautiful of Barbadian birds are the flower-loving humming birds whose wings vibrate at invisible speed as they flit from sip to sip of fragrant blossoms. Also beautiful though rare are the glossy blue male cowbirds. Pleasant voiced and also rare is the vireo. Fairly large and of piercing tones is the rain-bird or pee-whittler who loves to perch on telephone wires. All over Barbados, and inmates of most hotel dining-rooms, are the cheeky bull finches or brown sparrows who will not hesitate to sip your orange juice, peck your grapefruit or swallow your paw-paw if you dawdle on the way to breakfast.

More spectacular but also relentless in pursuit of sugar are the yellow-breasted banana quits, which some Barbadians know as 'moustache' birds. They especially patronise the trees of the Colony Club, trilling sweet songs until the sugar bowls appear, and they gather impatiently for 'lunch'. The first visiting birds from across the Atlantic, the long-legs arrive in early July in time for the local swamp bird shooting season. Swallows arrive in early September and leave in April. The big brown pelican comes and goes as the spirit moves him and from time to time a frigate or man-o'-war bird spreads his huge wings in flight across the sea. Other trans-oceanic water visitors have been Gargany teal, spitted redshank, wood sandpiper, jack snipe, European cuckoo, and alpine swift.

Most of the fruit, vegetables and ornamental trees which are seen in Barbadian gardens or on estates today were introduced from overseas. The Arawak Indians from Guyana brought cassava, maize (Indian corn), yams, peas, beans, plantains, bananas, oranges, lemons, limes, pineapples and melons. By 1631 pawpaws, water melons, pomegranates and figs were established. Within the next 20 years bonavist, cucumber and the tamarind tree were flourishing.

Coconut trees did not become common until the end of the seventeenth century, by which time the tangerine had been introduced from Portugal.

Captain Shaddock left the fruit named after him in Barbados when he called on a voyage from the Pacific in 1684.

The tomato was brought over from Portugal by Governor Worsley during the second decade of the eighteenth century and the breadfruit tree was successfully carried across the Atlantic to the West Indies by Captain Bligh in 1793. It was growing all over Barbados before the close of the century.

The casuarina, bamboo, mahogany and other shade trees were introduced into Barbados from overseas as were a great number of flowering trees.

The Barbados Pride was a very early import from the Cape Verde islands and was much used as a hedge on the plantations of the seventeenth century.

Trees flower mostly in Barbados between April and September. Among the most beautiful are the Rose of Sharon, the golden poui, the Queen of Flowers, the jacaranda, the frangipani, the flamboyant, the African tulip, the cordea and many varieties of cassia.

Popular vines are corallila and coralita, morning glory, bignonia, allamanda, chalice flower, onion vine, jessamine, and bougainvillaea of many hues.

Garden shrubs include dozens of colourful hibiscus, many shades of oleander, petreas, poinsettias, plumbagos, stephanotis, lagostroemia, ginger lilies, Ixora and Heliconia.

The highways and lanes of Barbados are often gay with multi-coloured crotons nodding in the breeze, acalyphas, eranthemums and other 'wayside' plants.

From time to time garden societies, the orchid society or Horticultural Society hold exhibitions of flowers and ornamental plants when visitors are always welcome. Sometimes the gardens of country homes are also opened in aid of local charities or under the auspices of the National Trust.

12 Food and Drink Through the Ages

Sir Henry Colt, writing to his son George in 1631, gives the earliest advice on diet suitable for a sea journey through the Caribbean. He was drawing on his own experience of a voyage to Barbados and St Christopher that year. 'Your stomach', he said, 'must be kept warm for digestion and to avoid the flux, the chiefest danger. Use pepper in all your broths and raisins of the sun eat morning and evening, it keeps you from thirst. Eat not much flesh, fruit or salt meats: oatmeal, peas, rice, wheat, butter and Holland cheese your best diet of all: a hen stewed with pepper and biscuit is good meat.'

His recipe for biscuits was to steep them in water three or four hours, then boil them in the same water. When the water was boiled away currants and pepper were added to the mixture, which was then buttered. Colt also recommended his son to buy white biscuits to eat in the morning with puddings of wheat flour mixed with raisins and buttered. He also approved of rounds of cod put in water the night before and boiled. When hard eggs and butter were added they provided 'one of the best meals at sea.'

For drinking before meals he recommended a little angelica water or rosemary. Aniseed water and aquavitae (at four shillings a gallon) might also be taken.

When he was in Barbados Colt heard that the settlers in the first years of settlement killed 1500 wild hogs a week for sport, leaving their bodies to rot on the ground. This folly had reduced the plentiful supply of meat, but some wild hogs were still hunted and Colt enjoyed a supper at Mr Futter's house where the table was loaded with 'pigs, capons, turkeys, chickens from the field, Indian wheat, cassava, and cabbages' from 200-feet-tall palm trees.

He also ate turtle during his stay, noting that the fat was

a dark yellow colour, while the flesh tasted like beef or veal. He also described their eggs as being 'round, white and soft without a shell, as big as hen's eggs'. The sea was 'well furnished with fish'. He caught so many with his own net that every mess in his ship got four apiece. Some were like pikes, some like mullets, others like sea bream. He was told that there were rats that 'eat in taste like young rabbits, but I eat not any yet'. The potatoes in Barbados were 'best of all others', the plantain was 'too sweet and dry', the pine of 'various tastes, most like unto a great white ripe strawberry, it is sweet, sharp, moist', the water melon was 'waterish and thaws in the mouth like ice with no other taste'.

Colt was most impressed by the 'marvellous swiftness' of 'air and soil' in the production of food. Wheat was made perfect in three months. Plants bore one year after they were put in the ground. Among those he saw were fig trees, vines, oranges, lemons, plantains, pomegranates, pines, Indian wheat 'red and white', the tree cassava for bread, peas, beans, guavas, the wild prickly apple (a pretty lively taste, the fruit great round and green), the pawpaw that carries a leaf like the fig tree but more jagged, and little and great pepper trees, which gave 'the best pepper in the world'. He also saw cows 'whose milk tastes better than in England', turkeys, peacocks, hens, wild hogs, English hogs, tame pigeons and wild pigeons.

'Only sloth and negligence could cause this people to want', Colt wrote later in his tent at St Christopher, for of 'all the islands I have passed by and seen unto this day, not any pleaseth me so well. Would it were my own, and thus seated in any part of Europe.'

He recommended the young men to 'bridle the excess of drinking' which inflamed their fiery spirits, but confessed that in a few days he followed their example. At this time 'beer' was sold in Barbados, but the drink most commonly used 14 years later when Ligon arrived was mobbie, which he likened to 'Rhenish wine in the must'. Mobbie was red if made from potatoes with red skins, otherwise white.

The potatoes were first washed in a tub and scrubbed clean with a broom. They were then transferred to a large brass pot in which water covered a 'quarter part of them'. A piece of doubled canvas or 'such cloth as sacks' was then fitted over the pot to prevent the escape of steam when the water boiled from a fire which was lit underneath. When soft the potatoes were taken out, they were squeezed and mashed very small in 'fair water', where they stayed for an hour or two until all the spirit of the roots was sucked out. The liquor and roots were then placed in a large bag, which resembled a jelly bag and was pointed at the bottom. Through this bag it dripped slowly into a jar, where it began to 'work' within two hours. It was allowed to stand for 24 hours before it was drunk. 'As you will have it stronger or smaller,' said Ligon, 'put in greater or lesser quantities of roots'. He did not commend its wholesomeness, however, because he believed it to cause 'Hydropic humours'.

The 'beer' which was taxed by Governor Hawley may have been perino, which Indians made from the cassava root after extraction of the poison. The poison was extracted in a most filthy manner. The Indians caused their 'old wives, who have small remainder of teeth to chew the root and spit out into water', where after three hours it was purged of the poisonous quality. Ligon's explanation of this strange phenomenon is utterly revolting. The 'poyson of the old womens breath and teeth', he wrote, 'having been tainted with many several poxes, are such opposites to the Cassavy, as they bend their forces so vehemently one against another, as they both spend their poysonous qualities in that conflict; and so the relict of them both, becomes less unwholesome; and the water, which is in itself pure, casts out the remainder of the ill qualities they leave behind: which is manifested by the extraordinary working, which is far beyond that of beer, wine, or sider with us in Europe. This drink will keep a month or two, being put into barrels, and tastes the likest to English beer of any drink we have here'. Today's visitor, who is unlikely to find perino anywhere, can find consolation instead from the mild, pleasant-tasting, locally-brewed beer.

Punch in Ligon's time was nothing like today's drink. It was made of water and sugar, became strong after standing for ten days and was 'fit for labourers'.

The plantain drink was made from peeled plantains which were mashed and boiled in water and then left to soak overnight. In the morning they were strained and bottled up. A week later the liquor was strong and pleasant, but had to be drunk sparingly because it was much stronger than sack and was 'apt to mount up into the head'.

Ligon described 'rum' without giving it a name. He called it a drink made of 'the skimming of sugar, which is infinitely strong, but not very pleasant in taste; it is common, and therefore the less esteemed; the value of it is half a crown a gallon, the people drink much of it, indeed too much, for it often layes them asleep on the ground, and that is accounted a very unwholesome lodging.' Far better for them to drink beveridge, which was made of spring water, white sugar and juice of oranges. 'This is not only pleasant but wholesome,' was Ligon's judgment on a drink which is still popular with Barbadians, who no longer call it beveridge.

For Ligon, however, the best drink that Barbados 'or the world affords is the incomparable wine of Pines'. It was certainly for him 'the Nectar which the Gods drunk; for on earth there is none like it; and that is made of the pure juice of the fruit itself, without commixture of water, or any other creature, having in itself a natural compound of all tastes excellent, that the world can yield. This drink is too pure to keep long; in three or four days it will be fine; 'tis made by pressing the fruit and straining the liquor, and it is kept in bottles'.

Besides the drink available on Barbados in 1647, imports then included English beer, French, Spanish and other wines from Madeira and Fiall (one of the Azores). Brandy, 'extreme strong but very wholesome', came from France, and England sent spirits made of aniseed, mint and wormwood.

Ligon claims to have taught the Barbadians the art of cookery, weaning them away from plain ways of boiling, roasting and sometimes baking to collops, hashes and fricassees. His appreciation of high living is unmistakable as he describes the two bills of fare he prescribes for an inland plantation and for one near the sea.

His first choice is Colonel James Drax's table on the very rare occasion when beef was served. The great 'regalio' for his fellow planters, comprises a boiled rump, a roasted chine, a large piece of roasted breast, baked cheeks, the tongue and part of the tripes minced for pies which are seasoned with sweet chopped herbs, suet, spice and currants, the leg pallets and other ingredients for an *olio podrido*, and a dish of marrow bones. When they have well eaten of this princely repast, another course is brought in, 'a potato pudding, a dish of Scots collops of a leg of pork, as good as any in the world, a fricassee of the same, a dish of boiled chickens, a shoulder of a young goat dressed with his blood and thyme, a kid with a pudding in his belly, a sucking pig, which is there the fattest, whitest and sweetest in the world, with the poignant sauce of the brains, salt, sage and nutmeg done with claret wine, a shoulder of mutton, which is there a rare dish, a pasty of the side of a young goat, and a side of a fat young shot upon it, well seasoned with pepper and salt, and with some nutmeg, a loin of veal, to which there wants no sauce being so well furnished with oranges, lemons and limes, three young turkeys in a dish, two capons, two hens with eggs in a dish, four ducklings, eight turtle doves and three rabbits; and for cold baked meats two Muscovia ducks larded and seasoned well with pepper and salt; and these being taken off the table another is set on, and that is of Westphalia or Spanish bacon, dried neats tongues, botargo, pickled oysters, caviare, anchovies, olives, and intermixed with these custards, creams, some alone, some with preserves of plantains, bananas, guavas put in, and those preserved alone by themselves, cheesecakes, puffs, which are to be made with English flour and bread; for the cassavie will not serve for this kind of cookery; sometimes tanzies, sometimes froises, or amulets, and for fruit, plantains, bananas, guavas, melons, prickled pear, anchove pear, prickled apple, custard apple, water melons and pines worth all that went before. To this meat you seldom fail of this drink mobbie, beveridge, brandy, kill devil, drink of the plantain, claret wine, white wine, and Rhenish wine, sherry, Canary, red sack, wine of Fiall, with all spirits that come from England.'

At Colonel Walrond's plantation near the sea at Fontabelle Ligon draws up a bill of fare similar in several ways to that of Colonel Drax's feast but lacking in sheep, goats and beef. Instead guests were offered mullet, mackerel, parrot fish, snappers red and grey, cavallos, terbums, crabs, lobsters, conyfish, and 'divers sorts more for which we have no names.' Colonel Walrond enjoyed the advantage of living 'not half a quarter of a mile from the sea' so that his cellars were kept stocked with wine of all kinds, oil, olives, capers, sturgeon, neats tongues, anchovies, caviare, botargo, and all sorts of salted meats, flesh and fish, such as beef, pork, English peas, ling, haberdine, cod, poor John and Jerkin Beef.

Ligon describes how the spirit he calls kill-devil was made. Small gutters conveyed the skimmings of the three lesser coppers down to the still-house, 'whereof the strong spirit is made which they call kill-devil, and the skimmings of the two great coppers are conveyed another way as worthless and good for nothing.' The liquid in the still-house only began to rise after it became a little sour and gave off a 'small liquor' called low wines. This liquor was put into the still and drawn off again. Of that, said Ligon, 'comes so strong a spirit, as a candle being brought to a near distance, to the bung of a hogshead or butt, where it is kept, the spirits will flie to it, and taking hold of it, bring the fire down to the vessel and set all a fire, which immediately breaks the vessel, and becomes a flame, burning all about it that is combustible matter.'

The apothecaries on the plantations prescribed a dram cup of this spirit for negroes suffering from cold or sickness. It was also given to Christian servants 'when their spirits were exhausted' by their hard labour and sweating in the sun, ten hours every day. It was retailed at the Bridge for local consumption and was also sold to ships for transport 'into foreign parts', and for drinking 'by the way'.

When drunk to excess 'kill-devil' made a man quarrelsome. Because a 'rumbullion' or tumult often resulted from drunkenness some people believe that rum got its name from this old Devonshire word which was frequently used in Barbados by Royalists who had escaped from England during the time of the Civil War. Another suggestion is that rum derives from the Latin word for sugar, *saccharum*. It is probable that the word 'punch' derived from the large puncheons or casks which were used to hold up to 120 gallons of liquid. In Barbados today a rum punch is a rum drink made of four parts of water, three parts of rum, two parts of falernum or other sweet syrup and one part of the juice of a local lime. To this mixture of 'one of sour, two of

35 and 36 (opposite) Fishing nets at Oistins, Christ Church. Below: Carlisle Bay and the highlands of the interior

sweet, three of strong, four of weak' is added a dash of Angostura bitter, a few grains of nutmeg and a sprig of mint.

A planter's punch has the same ingredients but is put in a long glass and is dressed with chunks of mango, pawpaw or other fruit in season. A slice of orange and a cherry on a toothpick are added for decoration. A common Barbadian drink, 'corn and oil', is a mixture of rum and falernum. Today's falernum is based on a 'concoction' mixed by a Barbadian, Henry Parkinson. It contained dried ground Barbadian almonds, brown sugar dissolved in water, finely ground cloves, ginger root and crushed limes. A descendant of Parkinson, Arthur Stansfeld, made use of this concoction when in 1934 he registered falernum as a trademark for a product marketed in the States and sold in Bridgetown.

The Bridgetown Club in Barbados still serves the most refreshing drink of sangaree, which was widely consumed by ladies and gentlemen throughout the West Indies for two centuries. Doctor Pinckard on a visit to Barbados in 1806 said that 'taken when parching with thirst from heat and fatigue', a draught of sangaree 'approaches nearer perhaps to god-like nectar than any other known liquor.' He added that a 'stronger sort of it is sometimes drunk under the superlative name of Sangorum'. Another traveller in 1830 found that in Barbados 'the indefatigable planter, the pleading barrister, the deciding judge, the attentive merchant and the laborious clerk all agree in the necessity of taking their quantum "of sangaree" with their second breakfast, adding "it is a right blessed drink in a warm country".'

A modern recipe for sangaree is: 'half fill a half pint tumbler with cracked ice, then add a wine glass of sherry, madeira or port, half a teaspoonful of syrup and half a teaspoonful of Curaçao or Dom. Fill the glass with soda water, add a slice of lime, stir and sprinkle a little grated nutmeg on the top'. A right blessed drink, but not beloved of Barbadian rum refiners.

Cockneys born within the sound of Bow Bells but living in Barbados on the 29th of October 1710 were present at a great feast held in a spacious room decorated with the arms of 12 companies of the City of London, and with pictures of Christ Church Hospital of Bethlehem, the Banqueting House at White-

37 (opposite) Aerial view of Sam Lord's Castle, built by a Regency buck and now a resort complex

ι

hall, the Royal Exchange, Gresham College, Temple Bar, the Monument and King William and Queen Mary.

Sideboard tables ran all round the room and were provided with 'glasses cisterns and basons'. In a letter to a friend in London a guest at the feast describes how 'by a mighty clangour of trumpets we had notice that dinner was coming up, when every man took his place with much quiet. The first course was served up in majestic order, and when we regaled ourselves pretty well and every man being armed with a mighty glass of wine the steward drank the Queen's health, which was followed by the rest of the company with the discharge of 25 guns. At the breaking up of the second course was drunk the Lord Mayor's health with prosperity of the City of London, with the discharge of 25 guns, muskets, etc. The two first courses were served up with flying streamers stuck in every dish with 'welcome' wrote on them in letters of gold. After several customary healths went round and every man had indulged himself in eating and drinking, the cloth was taken away and the table nobly furnished with all manner of liquors; when after 4 or 6 hours of hearty drinking the wise and sober went away, the more generous and bold stayed behind to play. Thus they diverted themselves by playing, drinking their friends' healths and firing of guns until midnight'.

George Washington, who was in Barbados during the months of November and December 1751, was frequently invited to dine in the houses of members of the Beefstake and Tripe Club which had been founded by Major Clarke. At Judge Maynards' the future first President of the United States saw the greatest collection of fruits he had yet seen on the table, including granadellas, sappodillas, pomegranates, sweet oranges, water melons, forbidden fruit, apples, guavas, etc. Later in his diary Washington expressed especial appreciation of the pine. He noted that half the land on plantations was growing food for the negroes. He mentioned guinea corn, yams, plantains, potatoes and rice.

Some planters, when Ligon arrived in 1647, were unable to afford bone meat more than twice a week and ate potatoes, loblolly (crushed maize boiled in water) and bonavist beans, on the remaining days. Servants only got meat if an ox died of natural causes, otherwise they lived on a diet of loblolly, bonavist or potatoes with water or mobbie for drink. Negroes hated loblolly, but enjoyed their weekly allowance of a bunch of plantains when they were in season.

Throughout the years the diets in Barbados improved and today residents have a fairly wide choice of meat, fish, vegetables and ground provisions which are grown locally and imported from abroad. A book published by the Child Care Committee of Barbados in 1964 gave 80 pages of recipes.

Cornmeal, breadfruit, yams, sweet potatoes, 'English' potatoes, white eddoes and rice are widely used in most households at different times of the year and are balanced by bonavist, kidney and Lima beans, pigeon peas, blackeyes, runcival and increase peas, beet tops, spinach, swiss chard, avocado pears, christophenes, egg-plants (aubergines), okras, pumpkins, squashes, cucumbers, tomatoes, beets, carrots, and sweet peppers.

Pumpkin, bonavist and eddoes are ingredients of popular soups while turtle soup is enlivened by a glass of sherry and a dash of local pepper wine. Barbadian households are seldom without hot sauce, a very strong condiment which 'roasts the tongue' but is lavishly applied to dishes of fried fish and baked pork. Among the ingredients are minced eschalot, onions, turmeric, ginger, mustard, salt, vinegar, bonnet peppers, horse radish and garlic.

Pepper wine results from placing 12 or 18 sliced small peppers to steep in white rum for a week or ten days. The mixture is then strengthened with Barbados white rum and a few drops will add piquancy to soup.

Although fried and steamed flying fish is popular with most Barbadians, who bemoan its scarcity and cost, in recent decades the most popular fish meal in the island is imported cod. And the most popular use of cod is in salt fish cakes, which are made from boiled and finely minced salt fish, to which boiled pumpkin and grated raw yam are added, the whole mixed up well with beaten eggs, milk, butter, salt and pepper, then made into cakes, dipped in breadcrumbs and fried in boiling lard. The smell of salt fish cakes still comes strongly on the evening breeze in certain streets of Bridgetown.

Also popular with Barbadians are sea eggs fried with chopped onions and sweet pepper until golden brown. Before cooking over a low heat for three minutes salt and pepper are thoroughly mixed in.

Pudding and souse is perhaps the oldest of all Barbadian special dishes. White or black puddings are made of grated sweet potatoes and pumpkin seasoned with thyme, sweet marjoram and eschalot tops; after salting the mixture is put into pigs' intestines thoroughly cleaned with lime juice. Black puddings are mixed in pigs' blood. There is a great art in cooking the puddings, which are tied at both ends with strings and hung to dip in boiling water where they are turned till cooked. So much attention is required that Barbadian housewives have a saying that unless the kitchen is quiet during cooking the puddings will burst. Souse is mostly made from the part of the pig which would otherwise not be eaten. It should be made from a young pig's head and feet. After boiling it is cut into pieces and placed in a bowl of brine containing lime juice and hot red peppers. It should be served with chopped onion, chipped or sliced cucumbers and cut peppers.

Barbadian women through the ages have learnt how to make good use of local fruit to make jams, jellies, sweets and ices. Among the sweets, coconut sugar cakes, guava cheese, shaddock rind and tamarind balls are still considered to be great delicacies.

Guava jelly, if not too sweet, is the purest of all preserves and is used with the flaming Barbados rum omelette, and on blancmanges as well as a substitute for marmalade. Barbados cherry jam is in some ways even more appetising than guava jelly, but is rarely seen outside private homes.

Among ices those made from coconut, guava, cherry and soursop are the most delicious and the most frequently served in hotels like Ocean View and Miramar, which have benefited greatly from the knowledge of Mr Victor Marson, perhaps the most expert man in the art of cookery to have lived in Barbados since Ligon laid the foundation of Barbadian cuisine.

13 Pirates, Treasure, Legends and the Supernatural

Henry Morgan, who became the 'admiral' of Mansvelt's pirate gang in the year 1666, was the child of a rich yeoman farmer in Wales. For services to the Stuart cause his uncle Colonel Edward Morgan was made Lieutenant-Governor of Jamaica in 1664. Henry was to fill this office himself in 1674 and was knighted for his services.

His apprenticeship in the West Indies had begun in Barbados. The exact date of his arrival is not known, but he took ship from Bristol as a young man in the belief that he was going to work for the man who sold him into bondage as soon as he set foot in Bridgetown. There is no record of the number of years Morgan stayed in Barbados before regaining his liberty. He may even have made influential friends there for he was commissioned by Sir Thomas Modyford, the Barbadian governor of Jamaica in 1668.

It seemed likely too that Morgan decided to go to Jamaica as soon as he learnt of his uncle's appointment as lieutenant governor there.

Morgan's departure from Barbados was natural for a man of his disposition. He was a man with few scruples and he and his boon companions looted, pillaged and raped mercilessly.

Much more surprising than Morgan's departure from Barbados was the stealthy exit of Major Stede Bonnet. Owner of a beautiful home, married and well educated, Major Bonnet does not conform to the average man's idea of an eighteenth-century pirate.

Writing in 1724, eight years after the Major had turned pirate, Captain Charles Johnson said that he was victim of a 'disorder of the mind', caused by 'some discomforts he found in a married state.' The inference is that life with Mrs Bonnet was worse than being an outlaw at sea. Whatever drove Major Bonnet

to act, he did, at his own expense, fit out a sloop called *Revenge*
with 10 guns and 70 men, in which he stole away from Barbados
one night. His first cruise off the Capes of Virginia resulted in
the plunder of several ships. But Bonnet's military title availed
him nothing at sea and because of his inexperience as a sailor
he came to an agreement with the pirate Edward Teach, better
known as Blackbeard. He soon found that he was 'out of the
frying pan into the fire'. Blackbeard's gang elected one of their
number, a certain Richards, to replace Bonnet as captain. Disillusioned, the Major began to think of early retirement in Spain
or Portugal. Blackbeard lost his ship soon afterwards and surren-
dered to the authorities. Major Bonnet sailed for Bath Town in
North Carolina where he received the King's pardon and got
clearance to sail to St Thomas for war duties. But the call of
piracy proved stronger than the call of duty in the King's service.
Under the name of Captain Thomas, the gentleman Major of
Bridgetown now 'recommenced a down-right Pirate by taking
and plundering all the vessels he met with'.

They were mostly sloops and snows trading between American
ports or running between Philadelphia, Barbados and Antigua.
Bonnet's richest haul was an Antiguan sloop carrying goods
valued at £500. But his career as a pirate was brief. He was captured by Colonel Rhet in Cape Fear river in the autumn of 1718.
He was imprisoned for nearly a month, escaped for a few weeks,
but was soon taken again. His trial before Nicholas Trot, Judge
of the Vice Admiralty and Chief Justice of South Carolina, lasted
until 12 November 1718. In sentencing the gentleman pirate of
Bridgetown the Chief Justice did not restrict himself to points of
law.

'I have just reason to fear,' he told Major Bonnet, 'that the
principles of religion that had been instilled into you by your
education have been at least corrupted, if not entirely defaced by
the scepticism and infidelity of this wicked age; and that what
time you allowed for study was rather applied to the Polite
Literature and the vain Philosophy of the times, than a serious
search after the Law and Will of God as revealed unto us in the
Holy Scriptures'.

Having passed sentence on the age, Nicholas Trot passed sentence on the Major but not before telling Bonnet that if he would

'now sincerely turn to Him, though late, even at the eleventh hour then He will receive you.' Although the Governor of South Carolina was prepared to send Bonnet for retrial in England, his 'friends' did not think the verdict would be any different there. Bonnet paid his debt to society reluctantly. Shortly before he was hanged by the neck he begged the governor to indent him 'as a menial servant to your Honour and this Government during my life and send me up to the farthest inland garrison or settlement in the country', promising too to reserve the use of his tongue 'to call continually on, and pray to the Lord, my God, and mourn all my days in sackcloth and ashes to work out confident hopes of my salvation at that great and dreadful day, when all righteous souls shall receive their just rewards'. There was no mention of Mrs Bonnet in this valedictory plea for mercy, but the lady, who seems to have been in some way responsible for her husband's late development as a pirate may have preceded Bonnet to the grave. The whole truth about Major Bonnet and his lady may never be known, but there is no doubt at all that he was guilty of no less than 13 piratical acts and that he killed no less than 18 persons while they were being committed.

For these deeds he is at least entitled to be considered as the most daring pirate known to the history of Barbados. His name is commemorated in the Bahamas on the M.V. *Stede Bonnet*.

Bonnet had made a clean break with his wife when he went to sea. Less admirable was the conduct of a gentleman by the name of Smitten. He and his wife lived unhappily together in 'The Grove', a house which once stood on Ridgeway plantation in St Thomas about a quarter of a mile from the parish church. According to the legend preserved by E. G. Sinckler, a police magistrate writing more than 60 years ago, Smitten's wife employed a young slave girl to spy on him during the visits he made to his mistress. Infuriated by this discovery of his illicit amours, Smitten made his slaves hang the girl spy on a calabash tree from which she was fortunately cut down in the nick of time on the orders of Smitten's wife. In revenge for being spied upon Smitten sold one of the plantations which had come to him through marriage and swore that she would never receive a penny for it. His plan was simple. He put all the money from the sale in a large wooden box which was then placed for protection in a leaden container. At dead of night with the the help of a slave he buried the box and got a slave to fix paving stones and cement them in place above his treasure. According to the legend he then shot the slave, happy in the knowledge that this felony, if discovered, would only cost him a £15 fine.

On Smitten's death a sealed envelope was found with instructions in his handwriting to the effect that if his will was opened before the lapse of 50 years, the bequests therein would become void and of no effect.

Smitten's cruelty to his wife seems to have been effective although no further reference is made in Sinckler's tale. He picks up the thread after 50 years had gone by since Smitten's death. Precisely then, he says, a foreigner arrived in Barbados from America by ship. He does not say who the foreigner was or why 50 years had to pass before his arrival. What is certain is that he had knowledge of Smitten's treasure. For the very first thing he did on coming ashore in Bridgetown was to hire a horse and buggy and drive out to The Grove, which was by then in a very dilapidated condition. His visit was most rewarding, for the very next morning the watchman on the plantation found that the paving stones of the porch had been dug up during the night, leaving a deep hole underneath, with the marks of a large box plainly visible. The foreigner was never seen again. We shall never know for sure how he learnt about the treasure.

No one knows exactly who originated the legend that the loot from the sack of Lima, including a Golden Madonna, was buried on the beach at Sandy Lane. But the story has persisted into modern times and searches for the treasure were made as recently as the 'fifties of this century, by a man who had achieved a reputation as a water diviner. He was not successful.

Stories of buried treasure have been common in Barbadian households for centuries and nearly every Barbadian child with imagination dreams of finding treasure from long ago. So hope of riches was quickly kindled in the mind of a young Barbadian when one day he found an old wine glass lying on the beach close to his house on the West Coast. He took the glass home and kept it as a prized possession. Many years later when he went to live in England he showed it to a medium.

The story, as I heard it, tells how the medium saw an island where coconut palms and casuarinas swayed in the trade winds. It was a coral island and no one was on the beach. But suddenly a ship appeared and dropped anchor. A small boat was immediately lowered into the sea and large trunks were brought on deck by sailors and taken down the gangway. After the boat was filled, the sailors jumped in and rowed ashore with their treasure. The medium next saw the sailors digging a large hole in which they later buried the trunks. It was high upon the sand on a spot which corresponded exactly to the one where our Barbadian had found his wine glass many years ago.

The coincidence encouraged the Barbadian to hope—but there was more to come. The medium went on to say that she saw the sailors opening a bottle of wine to celebrate the safe burial of the treasure. A moment later her voice rose in screams to describe a terrible fight in which every sailor was killed stone dead by the pirates. As her voice dropped back to its normal pitch before coming out of a trance she told the Barbadian that she could see the very glass he had brought with him tightly clutched in the fingers of one of the dead sailors.

What the medium saw in her trance left a lasting impression upon the Barbadian. For several decades he never returned to his island home, but not long after the end of World War II he went back to look after his property there. Hopefully he took across the Atlantic a mine-detector which he had acquired in London. As soon as was reasonable after his arrival he went down to the beach behind his family home where he had found the wine glass. He became wildly excited when he saw that the mine detector was registering the presence of metal below his feet. Quickly he organised a party of diggers and after three hours of strenuous work a pick struck steel. Childhood memories flashed through the mind of our treasure hunter. Golden goblets, precious stones, pieces of eight, doubloons and jewellery unlimited were about to be spread before his eyes.

The medium had seen *that* spot. It had to be there still. The diggers drove their picks into the sand in a frenzy of anticipation, picking their way with care around the metal which they had now exposed. Runnels of sweat coursed down their naked backs and fell on the sand. And then with one convulsive heave they prized the metal loose from the soil and raised it up. Peering through his misted spectacles our Barbadian treasure hunter then saw below him the buried chassis of one of the very earliest Ford cars to have been imported into Barbados. He never looked for treasure again nor consulted another medium, but lived to a ripe old age on the Mediterranean island of his choice.

The gruesome sailors who ate human flesh reached Barbados in January 1736 after being shipwrecked at sea on a voyage from Lisbon to Cutchoe in Guinea. In the second canto of *Don Juan* (LXXVII) Byron tells how

> *. . . such things as the entrails and the brains*
> *Regaled two sharks, who followed o'er the billow—*
> *The sailors ate the rest of poor Pedrillo.*

Simon McCone of Drogheda in Ireland and Thomas Thompson of Rhode Island, the only survivors of the ship *Mary*, made sworn statements in Bridgetown in February 1736 from which Sir Robert Schomburgk drew the account of their experiences in his *History of Barbados*.

The *Mary* had spent five months in Cutchoe getting a cargo of slaves, beeswax and ivory. The Captain of the *Mary* and his wife died in Cutchoe and William Rye was made captain. The ship then sailed for the Cape Verde islands. On the journey from the islands Rye died and the second mate, William Cook, was made captain. Four days later the ship sprang a leak, but as the captain was dead the damage could not be repaired. The leak grew larger and all hands were put to work pumping, even the slaves who were let free from their irons to help. But the leak still increasing 'we found,' said McCone and Thompson, 'we must prepare for the best we could, in our poor small boat, and so we went to work upon her, and put into her seven stone bottles of water and five bottles of brandy, which was all we could get; for when we had any provisions upon deck to throw into the boat, the slaves being in number two or three hundred and provisions being very short, they seized upon it, and eat it from us, and then the slaves got what liquor they could find; and perceiving us to be very much confused, they took the opportunity to get drunk and forsook the pump.

'We seeing this, and observing nothing but death likely to ensue, got into the boat, and veered her astern of the ship, the 8th of November 1735 at night, the ship being then upon sinking as we thought, and finding the rest of the ship's company wanted to jump into the boat, which must have sunk her, we remained astern not daring to pull alongside of the ship, which next morning we left to providence.

'Believing ourselves to be near the Canary islands, but to the leeward of them, we were obliged to bear away for some of the West India islands, which were at least five or six hundred leagues from us. Our boat's crew were two Portuguese, four English, one Irish and one Rhode Island man born. Fifteen white men we left aboard the ship, and which we believe perished with her.

'We sailed in the boat to and fro several weeks until the 8th of December last, to the best of our remembrance, at which time we saw a sail, which was a Snow, and which revived us all very much. We hoisted a signal of distress, and the Snow lay by, until we were so near her, that we could discern the men on the deck; and then she made sail and went away from us, without speaking to us, they being afraid, as we imagined, when they saw so many of us in the boat.

'Our hunger then being intolerable we were forced to kill one of our companions to eat, and so agreed together to begin with one of the Portuguese, whom we accordingly killed out of pure necessity, and cut his flesh in small pieces, and dipped it in salt until it was hard, and so eat it, though but very sparingly, and thus we were forced to do with four more of the crew out of the eight.

'We also killed the sixth man but were forced to do so because he would have killed me Simon McCone one of these declarators, for he struck me with the tiller of the boat, and had just bereaved me of life when this my comrade Thomas Thompson came to my relief, and we were forced thereof to kill him though we flung him overboard as we could eat no part of him.

'We the said Simon McCone and Thomas Thompson being the only survivors of all the crew that left the ship, were determined to live and die the one by the other, but to leave all things to the Almighty providence of God, expecting nothing less than famine; for we lived several days without eating anything save one small flying fish that flew into the boat and some small barnacles that grew on the boat which we were obliged to eat raw. At last we espied land which happened to be the island of Barbados where we had like to have been cast on shore, which was in January 1736, we being so extremely weak that we could not work the said boat. But Providence prevented it by a schooner, belonging to the said island, the Captain whereof Glanville Nicholas was so kind to take us up and land us at Bridgetown in the said island'.

A harrowing tale and a drama worthy of the notice of Lord Byron, who may have read of the incident in Dalzell's *Shipwrecks and Disasters by Sea*, or may have heard about it from Leigh Hunt whose family had connections with Barbados.

In his *Autobiography* Leigh Hunt tells of a song which was a favourite in his house because it referred to his father's birthplace. The lines he quotes are:

> *Come let us dance and sing*
> *While all Barbados bells shall ring.*

The words came near the end of the musical or operetta which George Colman the younger wrote after reading Steele's account of an Indian girl's romantic attachment to a young English merchant.

Ligon, the first historian of Barbados, knew the real girl Yarico as a slave in the house where he stayed. He describes her in his *History* as 'of excellent shape and colour, for it was a pure bright bay, small breasts with the nipples of a porphyric colour, this woman would not be wooed by any means to wear cloaths. She chanced to be with child, by a Christian servant, and lodging in the Indian house, amongst other women of her own country, where the Christian servants both men and women came; and being very great, and that her time was come to be delivered, loath to fall in labour before the men, walked down to a wood in which was a pond of water, and there by the side of the pond, brought herself abed; and presently washing her child in some of the water of the pond, lapped it up in such rags as she had begged of the Christians, and in three hours time came home with her child in her arms, a lusty boy frolic and lively.' 'This Indian,' continues Ligon,' dwelling near the sea coast upon the main, an English ship put in to a Bay, and sent some of her men ashore, to try what victuals they could find, for in some distress they were. But the Indians perceiving them to go up so far into the country, as they were sure they could not make a safe retreat, intercepted them in their return, and fell upon them, chasing them into a wood, and being dispersed there, some were taken, and some killed; but a young man amongst them straggling from the rest, was met by this Indian maid, who upon the first sight fell in love with him and hid him close from her countrymen (the Indians) in a cave, and there fed him, till they could safely go down to the shore, where the ship lay at anchor, expecting the return of their friends. But at last seeing them upon the shore, sent the long boat for them, took them aboard, and brought them away. But the youth when he came ashore in the Barbadoes, forgot the kindness of the poor maid that had ventured her life for his safety, and sold her for a slave who was as free born as he. And so poor Yarico for her love lost her liberty'.

Richard Steele, whose first wife, the widow Margaret Stretch owned property in Barbados which she had inherited from her planter father Ford, took up Yarico's 'cause' in number eleven of *The Spectator*. He saw nothing wrong in embellishing Ligon's simple tale. According to Steele's account, Yarico not only wore clothes but changed them frequently. Every day she wore a different dress ornamented with most beautiful shells, bangles and beads when she went to call upon her lover Thomas Inkle. She brought him gifts which had been conveniently presented by other lovers, skins of beasts and highly coloured feathers. At night she would lead him out of the cave to enjoy the natural Paradise of a tropical forest set amid the falls of waters where the melody of nightingales enkindled love. Then after many months of dalliance in this serpent-free Eden Thomas Inkle persuaded Yarico to board a ship for Bridgetown where the young Englishman sold the girl who saved his life, asking a very high price because she was with child.

Steele's imagination ran riot with Ligon's simple tale, but the story took on a new lease of life and was copied by other publications. Knox put it in his *Elegant Extracts* and Robert Burns read it in Marson's *Collections*. It even reached the continent of Europe in German translations. But the greatest event of all was the musical or operetta of George Colman the Younger which the Hunt family saw in London. The first performance was given at the Haymarket in 1787 with Mrs Kemble appearing as Yarico.

At least seven editions of the text were made over the next two decades. Colman gave free rein to his imagination. He introduced new characters and attributed Inkle's betrayal of Yarico to his designs upon Narcissa, the daughter of the governor of Barbados Sir Christopher Curry. But in keeping with the spirit of the times, which saw nothing wrong with a white man marrying a coloured girl, he makes Inkle repent of his 'folly' and keep faith with Yarico. Narcissa's fortunate suitor Captain Campley then bellows forth:

> *Come let us dance and sing*
> *While all Barbados bells do ring,*
> *Love scrapes the fiddle string*
> *And Venus plays the lute.*

After so rousing a chorus Yarico's final contribution sounds rather tame to modern ears, but was in tune with a romantic age:

> *Doomed to know care and woe*
> *Happy now is Yarico,*
> *Since her love will constant prove*
> *And nobly scorns to shrink.*

Much water had flowed since Yarico picked chigoes from Ligon's foot in Barbados. But true love had triumphed over prejudice and selfish ambitions.

If the tale of Inkle and Yarico is the greatest romance in Barbadian history, the Floating Jacket is its weirdest unsolved mystery.

More than 130 years ago there lived in St Philip's parish a fisherman, whose distinguishing dress was a coarse blue jacket, which he always wore when he went the rounds of houses distributing his catch. He was a good fisherman and housewives welcomed him at their kitchen doors. Then suddenly the supply of fish stopped and neighbours began to ask each other what had happened to the fisherman with the blue jacket.

Several weeks passed and then one morning a young man of the parish discovered a bundle of bloodstained clothes lying underneath a tree in a small copse. He reported his find to the authorities, but there was nothing to link the bundle with the missing fisherman because there was no body and no blue jacket.

The unsolved mystery of the missing fisherman in the blue jacket continued to puzzle the parishioners of St Philip for many a day until a second discovery was made. This time a labourer was walking home from work through the canefields which bordered on Mangrove and Ruby plantations. It was the rainy season and he discovered that a large pond had overflowed its banks. As he clambered onto high ground to avoid wading through the water he thought he saw an object floating in the middle of the pond. It was an overcast day and the pond reflected the dark colouring of the sky, but he was able to identify the object as a jacket with outstretched blue sleeves.

Anxious to be the first man to tell the news he ran as fast as his legs would carry him towards the house of a planter who was also a justice of the peace. The justice and some of his friends were in the front gallery of his house stretched out in Berbice and rocking chairs sipping rum and falernum when they saw the man staggering up the drive. Quickly they rushed down the double stone welcoming steps to hear the man stutter out his tale of the jacket he had seen floating in the pond. The justice gave the man a drink and invited him to go back with him and his friends. The jacket was still visible when they got there but within a minute it sank and disappeared from view. By now a large crowd of curious persons had gathered at the pond and the justice of the peace persuaded some of the younger boys to swim out and see if they could find the jacket under the water. In the few remaining minutes of daylight the young men swam and dived around the centre of the pond, but had found nothing when darkness fell and the justice called off the search.

The next day early in the morning the justice of the peace took out a new search party equipped with a small Moses boat which a mule cart drew up from the Crane beach. The news of the floating jacket had spread all over the parish during the night and hundreds of persons were grouped around the pond when the search party arrived. The low murmurs of conversation suddenly ceased and were followed by a frightened silence as the blue jacket floated upwards and lay with sleeves outstretched in the middle of the pond. Then pandemonium broke loose, women bawling 'Lord have mercy' while old crones screamed 'Obeah. Obeah'.

Unperturbed by the terror of the onlookers the justice of the peace pushed his way forward towards the boat which had been placed by the water's edge and gave orders for his men to row out to the floating jacket. In a few swift strokes they had reached the spot where it lay, but the eddies from the oars or some mysterious agency sucked the jacket under the water and it quickly disappeared from sight as the people ashore began to shout and scream 'Obeah! Obeah!'

The men in the boat prodded the water with their oars for more than an hour, but they discovered nothing. So the justice of the peace called off the search and went away to draw up plans for the next day. The crowd waited for hours but when they saw nothing happen drifted off to their homes to discuss the floating jacket and the evil that the obeah workers would bring upon St Philip if the fisherman's body was not discovered.

By noon next day the canefields were alive with thousands of people who had come from all over the island to see the mysterious blue jacket. The sun was overhead and its rays beat fiercely down on the heads of the men and women waiting patiently for the jacket to appear. Then precisely at noon it obligingly rose to the surface and floated comfortably over the middle of the pond. Before the crowd had begun to scream and shout their imprecations of 'obeah' swimmers and divers leapt into the pond and swam out towards the jacket, but once again it sank before they could lay their hands upon it.

The crowd was by now thoroughly frightened, and the old crones of St Philip began to throw their heads up to the heavens prophesying terrible disasters for Barbados if the fisherman's body could not be found. People's tongues wagged unceasingly as the tale of the disappearing blue jacket passed from parish to parish to reach eventually the ears of the Royal Governor in his residence at Pilgrim House.

By noon the next day His Excellency, escorted by a troop of mounted soldiers carrying muskets, joined tens of thousands of Barbadians who since morning had taken up position in the canefields near the pond to wait for the jacket's daily noontime appearance. The justice of the peace was early on the scene and had four boats stationed in the pond ready for action as soon as the jacket was seen.

Promptly at noon it rose and settled, sleeves outstretched in the centre of the pond, but as soon as the oars began to splash in the water it sank from sight.

The governor now took charge and ordered the boats to come back ashore. As soon as the men stepped out the jacket rose again to the surface. Immediately the governor gave his musketeers the order to fire. Bullets whistled across the water and riddled the jacket with holes. The governor ordered the musketeers to cease firing and sent the boats out to recover the jacket. But before the boats could reach the middle of the pond the jacket sank from sight for the last time.

No further searches were attempted until the end of the rainy season when the pond dried up. The justice of the peace then conducted a thorough search of the ground but not a stitch of cloth was found.

The body of the fisherman was never found and no one can say for certain that the jacket in the pond was his. Other bodies, even in this century, have disappeared completely from Barbados without leaving any trace. If the fisherman had been the victim of a murder it is possible that the murderer buried the conspicuous jacket in the pond and that it floated to the surface after heavy rains. Speculations about the mysterious behaviour of the jacket at this distance of time is unrealistic, but one theory which would explain all the facts of the legend is that the murderer might have been one of the rescue party and always the first man to reach the jacket so that he could push it beneath the surface. When the search was finally abandoned after the shooting of the jacket by the soldiers, he would then have had the opportunity to remove the jacket drilled full of holes from the bottom of the pond before it dried up at the end of the rainy season.

The readiness of Barbadian villagers to accept as gospel truth any old wives' tale is illustrated by the experience of a young Barbadian doctor in the late 'forties of this century. An old man had died and was buried in the churchyard of St Barnabas. Soon after the funeral, someone, who could have been a relative overcome by grief, told a friend that he had heard a knocking coming from the old man's grave. Several people in Barbados at the time could remember the tales told about hundreds of persons who had been carted away for dead during the cholera epidemic and

M

who were buried alive. In my own childhood I had been told how a rich woman who died in that epidemic woke up in her coffin to find two thieves attempting to cut off the fingers on which she wore her rings. She frightened them out of their wits by asking them in a quiet voice to 'take the rings' but 'spare the finger'.

The horror of being buried alive is deep rooted in many and the people of St Barnabas were terrified at the thought that one of their late neighbours might be lying under the ground near to them begging to come back to life. The next day the rumour that the old man was still alive gained ground and reached the ear of a police officer. Two days later the authorities granted permission for an exhumation to be carried out in the presence of a doctor. Although the doctor sensibly pointed out that even if the man had been alive when he was buried he would surely have been suffocated by the third day, the police insisted on his being present at the exhumation. When he arrived to conduct his investigation the crowds had assembled in their thousands to see whether the dead man would come out of the coffin alive. The police had to clear the way for the doctor to reach the grave. Then with stethoscope around his neck he clambered down into the open hole. There he found the corpse of an old man of 70 lying contentedly in his final resting place. Once the doctor had certified the man to be dead the people were satisfied. They drifted back to their rumshops and cottages to discuss the true story of the man who had knocked on his coffin after burial, but who was now safely dead and buried.

Many people alive in Barbados today have a firm belief in ghosts and spirits who visit from another world. Some claim to have seen dead people revisit scenes of their past life, while others have awakened to find their furniture thrown all over their living-rooms by poltergeists. I know one solid citizen who claims that her house was visited by poltergeists during three successive Februaries. She no longer lives there.

As a child I was much impressed by the tale of a helpful ghost who had departed this life by committing suicide in a three-storied house near Bridgetown. He was found hanging from a hook in the ceiling. According to my informant a lady who lived in this house some years after the suicide had been working all day downstairs in the kitchen and being very tired was dreading the climb up three flights of stairs to her room. As she put her foot on the first step she found herself saying 'Oh dear, I wish I had someone to give me a lift upstairs'. The words were still on her lips when a powerful arm clutched her waist and lifted her right off her feet. When she had recovered from the shock she found herself standing outside her bedroom at the top of the house.

Several Barbadian homes besides Sam Lord's Castle are said to be haunted. Old Joe's River Plantation House in St Joseph was, according to tradition, haunted by ghosts and was the setting for two murders and a burial. The story begins with the death of the owner of the plantation. He left his son in the care of a brother. This man killed the young heir and his nurse and took the estate for himself. He was so wicked a man that after his death his horses refused to drag his coffin to the cemetery. They kicked their feet up in the air and became so unruly that the body was taken from the hearse and buried in the estate yard. Nothing seems to have happened until some years later new tenants moved into the house and complained of seeing the ghosts of a little boy and his nurse. The apparitions continued for some days until workmen were hired to knock down a wall which the wicked uncle had constructed soon after the murder to seal off the bedroom of the heir. The spirits of the child and his nurse were then apparently satisfied that the house had been restored to its normal state and were seen no more.

St Joseph's parish is the setting for another story of the supernatural. One Friday the rector of the parish church had travelled to Bridgetown with his son to do their weekly shopping. On the way back they had reached Malvern estate, where the son worked as manager, when a terrific thunderstorm broke and lightning streaked across the sky. Alarmed for his wife who was alone at home, the rector resisted the pleas of his son to spend the night with him at Malvern and set off alone in the trap. He had only travelled a few yards when the lightning ceased and the rain began to fall in blinding torrents of water.

Neither horse nor driver could see where they were going. Then all at once a piercing flash of lightning lit up the darkness accompanied by an ear-splitting clap of thunder which made the horse pull up dead in his tracks. The rector, wiping the rain from his eyes as he peered ahead, saw right in front of him a thousand-foot precipice. He was on the verge of leaping out to pull the horse back to safety when a figure appeared from nowhere and began to lead the horse safely back on to the road which led down-hill to the rectory. On arrival the rector searched in his purse for a silver coin with which to reward the good samaritan, but when he got out the guide had disappeared. Whenever the rector told this story afterwards he said that it was his guardian angel who had led him safely home that night.

Unlike ghosts, poltergeists and guardian angels, who are regarded as visitors from the world beyond the grave, men and women who make obi are commonly thought of as workers of magic or as adept in witchcraft. For years in Barbados there lived an old white woman who enjoyed the reputation of being a real witch. She lived near the beach at Cattlewash in St Joseph and was consulted by persons who believed in her powers. Taxi drivers pointed out her house to curious visitors as one of the sights of Barbados.

The practice of obi, however, was predominantly African in origin and the Ashanti word Obayifo is translated into English as wizard or witch. 'Making obi' in the West Indies was a means of livelihood for persons who exploited African skills which gave those who possessed them enormous influence over those persons who believed that their powers were supernatural. Although originally connected with ancient religious practices in Africa the practice of obi in the West Indies has mainly been concerned with providing cures for sickness or disorder, concocting schemes for revenge or granting of favours, exposure of thieves or adulterers, and foretelling the future.

In a report relating to Trade and Foreign Plantations published in 1789, the Council of Barbados states that Obeah 'has been so long known here that the origin is difficult to trace, but the professors are as often natives as Africans.'

Obeah practices were common in Barbados during the centuries of slavery and have not yet died out. Because the deaths of many slaves were caused by poisoning any one who was convicted of making obi was liable to a penalty of death in the eighteenth century.

White men as well as black feared the power of the obi makers.

Many an overseer and master are known to have left Barbados under the impression that they had been 'bewitched'. Even in the 'fifties of this century I knew of one Englishman who flew out of Barbados under the firm conviction that someone had 'worked obi' against him. And it is still possible to see in Barbados today someone wearing a piece of red rag around the neck or arm as a precaution against the threats of an obi worker. So common is the fear of obeah that some people do extraordinary things to escape their power. My wife once discovered a maid in the act of burning her kapok pillow while drinking white rum and garlic. When asked what she was doing she said she was killing the obi a St Lucian servant had put in her pillow which made the fibres turn into snakes which bit her while she slept at night.

A very terrible fear comes over the person who is given a match box containing a dead lizard. Also dreaded is discovery of a small bottle containing filthy fluid, feathers or other concoctions.

An immediate action is to make the obi turn against the sender. This is done by throwing the object away and letting it be known that you have got a more powerful obi which has been put to work. Catholic priests are believed by obi workers to have a stronger obi than ordinary practitioners, but this belief did not prevent an obi worker from sending several dead chickens through the post to the rectory of a priest whose cook was the intended victim.

Obeah was perhaps most closely studied by a priest Father Emerick when he spent 11 years in Jamaica. He regarded it as a combination of magic and witchcraft. His conclusions are valid for Barbados. Obi men, he said, were of all sorts, just as 'you have professional doctors and quack doctors.' 'Any rascal,' he said, 'who wants to gratify his revenge, avarice or lust can work upon the superstitious, practice obi and get a following as an obi man.' He describes 'obeahism' as a form of religion and says that 'His Satanic Majesty is the invisible head of Obeah'. The obi man's incantation was muttering of strange sounds with no particular meaning, pronouncing of words over the objects to be 'obeahed' and performance of grotesque actions. Among the objects he kept by him were lizard skins, rum, parrot's tongues, eggs, chicken heads, dirt from a graveyard, cat claws, feathers and dried leaves.

Sometimes confused with obeah practices is mialism. The mial man is adept at depriving persons of their shadows or 'souls'. Once a person has lost his shadow he pines away and dies. The only remedy is for his shadow to be caught again by another mial man. A description of shadow catching is given by Father Emerick in a privately printed book. Invariably it is done at night. The person suspected of having lost his shadow is taken to the cotton tree, where his shadow is spellbound or to which it is nailed. A large group of people attend the ceremony. The victim is dressed all in white with a white handkerchief about his head. Eggs and fowls are taken together with food, to the cotton tree. The mial men and women parade up and down before the cotton tree with white cloths over their shoulders singing and dancing, and all the people join in the chorus. The cotton tree is pelted with eggs and the necks of fowls are wrung off and the bodies are cast at it. This is done to propitiate the deaths or duppies that had their shadows enthralled at the tree. The singing and dancing proceed more vigorously as the shadows begin to make signs of leaving the tree. A white basin of water to receive it is held up. After they have sung and danced to their hearts' content, they suddenly catch up the person and run home with him, affirming that his shadow is caught and covered up in the basin. When the patient has reached his home, a wet cloth is applied to his head and his shadow is said to be restored to him.'

In Barbados the word 'mialism' is never heard, but the silk cotton tree is often spoken of as the tree of duppies and many people alive in Barbados would be terrified to lose their shadows. In the Barbados Museum you can see a Trinidad obeah coffin which was once used to catch a victim's shadow. It is a little larger than three and a half inches and over one inch wide. On it is scratched a 'duppy cat' and a setting sun as symbol of death.

Religion, education, travel and higher living standards have diminished the hold of superstitious beliefs upon today's Barbadians, but memories of the past linger on in daily speech and at times revive to plague those who are fearful.

Chronology

1529   Barbados marked on map of the world.
1563   Visit by Pedro a Campos. Introduction of hogs.
1625   Visit of the *Olive Branch*. Cross set up near Holetown.
        'James K. of E. and of this island' carved on tree.
1627   February. Captain Henry Powell brought first tobacco
        planters in *William and John*.
        Grant of Carlisle Province to James Earl of Carlisle.
1628   Arrival of Carlisle's tobacco planters.
        Grant of Montgomery Province to Philip, Earl of
        Montgomery.
        Second grant of Caribbees to Carlisle. Barbados identi-
        fied as one of Caribbees.
1629   Lord Keeper's judgment in favour of Carlisle.
        Hawley appointed Governor.
1631   Privy Council regulate and limit tobacco growing on
        plantations.
1639   Hawley sets up republican régime in Barbados and
        'settles a parliament', which chose him as governor.
1640   Hawley deposed by commissioners.
1642–50 Rule of Governor Bell.
        Planting of sugar cane and establishment of mills and
        boiling houses for manufacture of sugar.
1647   Lord Willoughby of Parham appointed Lieutenant
        General of Caribbee islands.
        Plague in Barbados.
1648   Rule of 'the Rump' in England.
1649   30 January. Execution of Charles I.
        Royalist *coup d'état* in Barbados. Republicans expelled.
1650   Royalist councillors and assemblymen in Barbados
        proclaim Charles II as King of England, Scotland, France,
        Ireland, Barbados and all other plantations. Rump par-
        liament pass Navigation Act.

1651　Sir George Ayscue ordered to reduce Barbados to the obedience of the Commonwealth.

1652　June. Republicans obtain control of Barbados after signing of article of agreement known as the Charter of Barbados.

1653　March. Cromwell marched troops into House of Commons and expelled members.

December. Cromwell becomes Protector.

1654　Cromwell decides to launch his Western Design.

1655　Venables 'overlord' of Caribbees and plantations arrived in Carlisle Bay on 28 January. Sets up headquarters of Western Design.

31 March. Venables and over 7,000 soldiers, sailors and nurses left Barbados for Hispaniola in 60 ships.

1656　Boom year for Barbados sugar exports.

1660　Restoration. Death of second Earl of Carlisle. House of Assembly elected annually from this year.

1660–70　Decade of poor sugar crops due to soil exhaustion, droughts and attacks by insect pests.

1661　Assembly pass act 'for the better ordering and governing of negroes'.

1662　Lord Willoughby appointed Governor of Caribbees.

1663　Abolition of feudal rights over Barbados.

Assembly agrees to imposition of $4\frac{1}{2}\%$ duty on all dead commodities grown or produced in Barbados.

Parliament passes act to compel all foreign imports to pass through England as a staple.

1665　April. Dutch Admiral De Ruyter destroys buildings in Bridgetown during attack by sea.

1666　Lord Willoughby drowned off Isle des Saintes.

1667　Sir Tobias Bridge appointed commander of military forces in Barbados.

Leewards ask King to be 'no longer under the government of Barbados'.

1668　House of Assembly asks for 'dominion status' for Barbados.

Over 100 houses burnt in Bridgetown fire. Damages exceed £30,000.

Crops ruined by drought.

1673	Slaves classified as real estate, instead of chattels. Negroes armed for service in militia.
1675	Destructive hurricane, 31 August.
1680	Comprehensive census of Barbados made by Governor Sir Jonathan Atkins.
1685	James II's sugar tax. Drop in sugar prices.
1688	James II driven from throne.
1689	Edward Littleton's *The Groans of the Plantations*.
1691	Assembly appoints agents in London (until 1848).
1694	Over 40 sugar plantations abandoned.
1695	British regiment sent as garrison to Barbados.
1697	House of Assembly made itself a House of Commons. Act repealed in UK.
1703	Monthly sailing packet established between England and West Indies.
1710	Assembly authorised by Queen to appoint Treasurer of island.
1712	English slave ships granted equal rights to African trade.
1722	Bishop of London extends jurisdiction to British colonies.
1731	First Barbadian newspaper, the *Barbados Gazette*, published by David Harry and Samuel Keimer.
1740	Freemasonry founded by Alexander Ervine.
1745	Jacobite prisoners shipped to Barbados after Culloden.
1754	Act to reduce rate of interest to 6%.
1765	Stamp Act imposed on Barbados. £2,500 paid before repeal in following year. Moravian mission begun.
1766	Speaker formally claimed privileges for members of House of Assembly. Bridgetown twice destroyed by fire.
1780	Only 3 churches escape destruction in the great hurricane which reduced Bridgetown almost to ruins. Valuable registers lost.
1782	April. Rodney's victory over de Grasse established British supremacy in West Indies.
1789	Wesleyans build first 'preaching hounse' in Barbados.
1804	Proposal to allow free coloured to give evidence in courts refused. Not granted till 1817. Barbados merchants commission frigate to protect coasts.

N

1805   23 December. Illuminations to celebrate Nelson's victory at Trafalgar.

1810   Silver mace provided for House of Assembly, silk gown for Speaker.

1812   Dust from St Vincent's volcano caused 6 hours of darkness over Barbados.

1812–14 Naval engagements off Barbados against US ships.

1816   Bussa's Rebellion. Negro slave leaders transported to British Honduras.

1823   Destruction of Wesleyan chapel in Bridgetown. Preacher Shrewsbury fled to England.

1825   First bishop of Barbados, Dr Coleridge, arrived in January.

1826   Chief Justice Renn Hampden sentenced John Archer, a white man, to a year's imprisonment for manslaughter. First verdict to establish right of a slave to protection under the common law.

1827   First steamship arrived in Barbados.

1831   Hurricane killed over 2,000 persons and destroyed much property. Political disabilities of Jews, free coloured and free black people removed.

1833   Governor's salary paid from imperial funds.

1834   Slavery abolished.

1835   Establishment of Police Force.

1838   1 August. Emancipation day to celebrate abolition of 'apprenticeship' for all labourers.
Abolition of $4\frac{1}{2}$% duty by UK Parliament.
Assistant Court of Appeal established.

1840   General Hospital established by private subscriptions.

1841   Permanent Chief Justice appointed.

1843   Constituency of Bridgetown elects two representatives to Assembly for first time.
Samuel Jackman Prescod first coloured man to be elected.

1845   Ten acres of Bridgetown destroyed by fire.
Barbados proposed as capital of five Windward Islands.

1846   General Agricultural Society founded.
UK Parliament passes 'Sugar Duties Act'.

1847   Commercial panic.

1848	Currency assimilated to that of UK.
1852	Savings Bank established. Inland post offices set up. First lighthouse erected at South Point.
1854	20,000 people died of cholera.
1858	First agricultural exhibition held at Government House. First issue of Barbados stamps.
1860	Destructive fire in Bridgetown near Trafalgar Square.
1861	Waterworks established in Bridgetown.
1866	Canadian Trade Mission to Barbados.
1867	Harbour Police formed. Joined to land police force in 1882.
1872	Opening of Swing Bridge and Public Buildings West Wing. Hydrophobia act. First telegram received on 7 March.
1875	Bridgetown first lit by gas.
1876	Confederation Riots.
1878	Elementary education introduced.
1881	Executive Committee introduced in Executive Council.
1882	Completion of Barbados railway, Bridgetown to Belleplaine.
1884	Proposal for Barbados to join Canadian Federation.
1885	Barbados separated from government of Windward Islands.
1886	Piped water extended to rural districts.
1898	Violent storm destroyed large numbers of wooden houses and took 100 lives.
1897–1910	Expansion of agricultural education. Diversification of crops.
1903	March. Volcanic ash from Soufrière volcano in St Vincent blows over Barbados.
1944	Extension of franchise.
1946	Bushe experiment in 'cabinet' government.
1951	Introduction of adult suffrage.
1954	Inauguration of ministerial government.
1958	Full cabinet government.
1958–62	Barbados united with Federation of West Indies.
1966	30 November. Barbados achieves independence within the Commonwealth. The Queen continues to be Queen of Barbados.

Major Wars of England and Empire from 1627–1945

1627–9   War against France
1642–6   First Civil War
1648   Second Civil War
1649   Conquest of Ireland begun
1650–51 Scots conquered at Dunbar and Worcester
         Prince Rupert's fleet destroyed.
1652–4   First War against Dutch.
1655–59 War against Spain.
1665–7   Second Dutch War
1672–4   Third Dutch War
1685   Monmouth Rebellion
1690   William III defeats Irish forces at the Boyne
1689–97 War of the League of Augsburg against France
1701–13 War of the Spanish Succession against France and Spain
1739–48 War against Spain and from 1744 against Spain and
         France
1756–63 War against France and from 1762 against Spain
1775–83 War against America and from 1778 against France
1793–1802 War against France.
1803–15 War against France and from 1808 till 1812 in Spain
1812–14 War against United States
1816–18 Central India conquered
1824–26 First Burmese War
1837   Rebellion put down in Canada
1839–41 Afghan War
1840–42 War against Chinese. Hong Kong annexed
1854–6   War against Russia
1878   Second Afghan War
1879   Zulu War
1899–1902 Boer War
1914–19 First World War
1939-45 Second World War

Note: Barbados was indirectly involved in all these wars as a
      dependency of Britain and contributed to several through
      taxes, defence expenditures, raising of troops and in other
      ways. Wars also affected trade, often unfavourably.

Bibliography

Three stock histories of Barbados have in recent years become available as reprints in the Cass Library of the West Indies.

The earliest detailed information about the island comes from Richard Ligon's *A True and Exact History of the Island of Barbados*, which was first published in 1657.

Another history by John Poyer was published in 1808. It is principally influenced by an account of Barbados in the forty-first volume of the Universal History and by Hall's account of the First Settlement of Barbados. The author also had access to proceedings of the House of Assembly, private papers and two unpublished manuscripts. The chief merit of Poyer's history is that he wrote as a native of the island. His description of the awful hurricane of 1780 still has power to move modern readers. This history was reprinted in 1971, and is especially valuable for eighteenth-century Barbados.

Sir Robert Schomburgk's *The History of Barbados* is more than a history. It gives the first geographical and statistical description of the island and relates its geology and natural productions. The illustrations, which were drawn on stone, have especial value today as records of what Barbados looked like in the year 1847, when Schomburgk wrote. The book was reprinted in 1971.

Neville Connell's *A Short History of Barbados*, published by the Barbados Museum and Historical Society, is by contrast a very slim condensation of 300 years of life on the island. Its value is nonetheless great as an introduction.

Some useful documents relative to early Barbados are to be found in Eric Williams' *Documents of West Indian History 1492–1963*, published in Trinidad in 1963 by the PNM Publishing Company.

Two recent books by American authors probe deeply into the

social structure of the island during the seventeenth century. They are *No Peace Beyond The Line*, by Carl and Roberta Bridenbaugh (Oxford University Press, New York, 1972), and *Sugar and Slaves*, by Richard S. Dunn (Jonathan Cape, 1973).

Vincent Harlow's *A History of Barbados 1625–1685* (Oxford, 1926) and James A. Williamson's *The Caribbee Islands under the Proprietary Patents* (Oxford, 1926) remain the two most important historical studies of early Barbados by English historians.

Perspectives of war and trade are brilliantly portrayed by Richard Pares in *War and Trade in the West Indies 1739–1763* (London, 1963) and *Yankees and Creoles* (London, 1956).

Lowell Ragatz's *The Fall of the Planter Class in the British Caribbean 1763–1833* (New York, 1963) and Eric Williams, *Capitalism and Slavery* (London) assess varying roles of Barbados during the rise decline and fall of the plantation economies.

Interesting flashlights on the island are to be found in Sir Alan Burn's *History of the West Indies* (London). These are told in chronological order and are fitted into the main story of all the islands from settlement to modern times.

The West Indian Islands (Batsford,1972) by George Hunte puts Barbados into a pattern of islands running from Tobago in the south to Puerto Rico in the north.

Index